HOLIDAY

AGES 11-12

Contents

Into Year 7

Tear out these pages before you begin.

First published 1998

Letts Educational, Aldine House, Aldine Place, London W12 8AW
Telephone: 0181-740 2266

Text:	© BPP (Letts Educational) Ltd 1998
Authors:	Ann Broadbent
	Peter Chrisp
	Louis Fidge
	Hilary Koll
	Anneli McLachlan
	Steve Mills
	Judith Morris
	Gill Munton
	Myra Murby
	Graham Peacock
Consultant:	Judith Morris
Concept development and project management:	Myra Murby
Design and illustrations:	© BPP (Letts Educational) Ltd 1998
Concept design and cover:	Tessa Barwick
Production design:	Kim Smith (PDQ Reprographics)
Illustrations:	Alan Batley
	Robin Carter
	Lucy Holmes
	Claire Littlejohn
	Vanessa Lubach
	Coral Mula
	Bill Piggins
	Andy Pritchett
	Kim Smith
	Tim Stevens
	Michaela Stewart

All the authors are teachers and educationalists who have written many successful educational titles.

British Library Cataloguing in Publication Data
A CIP record for this book is available from the British Library.

ISBN 1 85758 787 1

Printed by Sterling Press
Reprographics by PDQ Reprographics, Bungay, Suffolk NR35 1EF

Letts Educational is the trading name of BPP (Letts Educational) Ltd.

HOLIDAY is packed with exciting activities, projects and stories for the summer.

It will build your brainpower for Year 7.

This book will help you in:

Reading

Writing

Maths

Science

History

Geography

General knowledge

Art & craft

French, German and Spanish

Have fun this summer!

Ask a grown-up to pull out the pages at the back.

SOURCES FROM HISTORY

Dating the past

The letters BC and AD are used as a way of dating events in the past. BC means 'before Christ' – before the birth of Jesus Christ, almost two thousand years ago. AD means 'Anno Domini' (the year of the Lord), or years after the birth of Christ. So 20 BC means 20 years before the birth of Christ. AD 20 means 20 years after the birth of Christ.

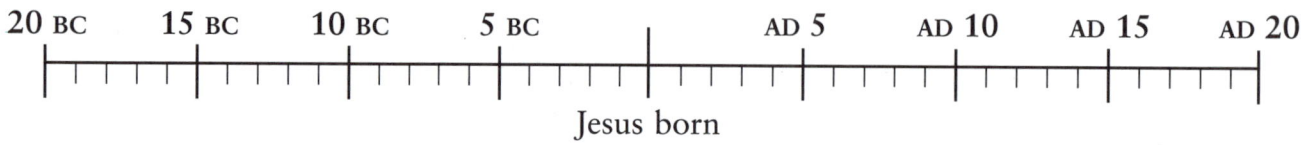

20 BC   15 BC   10 BC   5 BC   AD 5   AD 10   AD 15   AD 20

Jesus born

When we talk about the year 2,000, we mean AD 2,000 – two thousand years after the birth of Christ. How many years after the birth of Christ were you born? _____

Julius Caesar comes to Britain

In 55 and 54 BC, a Roman general called Julius Caesar made two expeditions to Britain. We know this from letters and books written by Roman writers, including Caesar himself. Historians call such writings *sources*. Read each of these sources carefully, then answer the questions on the next page.

Julius Caesar

Source A

'Caesar's expeditions were wonderfully daring. He was the first person to take a Roman army across the sea to Britain. At the time, many writers said that this island did not really exist. They said that the stories about Britain were all made up! Caesar fought several battles but did not conquer the island. He found that the Britons were so poor and wretched that there was nothing worth taking from them.'

Plutarch, *Life of Caesar*
(written AD 110-20)

Source B

'Caesar got nothing for Rome from Britain except the glory of having led an expedition there. Indeed he took great pride in this.'

Dio Cassius, Roman History (written around AD 200)

Source C

'I hear there's no gold or silver in Britain. If this is so, I advise you to get a war-chariot and hurry home to us as soon as possible.'

Cicero, letter from Rome to a friend in Caesar's army, June 54 BC

Source D

'We're eagerly waiting to find out how the war in Britain turns out. But it seems likely that there's nothing to be got there except slaves.'

Cicero, letter from Rome to a friend, July 54 BC

Source E

'The most civilised Britons are those who live in Cantium (Kent). Most of those who live inland do not grow crops. They live on milk and meat and wear skins. All Britons dye themselves blue with the woad plant, which makes them look terrifying in battle. They wear their hair long and shave their bodies, except for the upper lip.'

Julius Caesar, The Gallic War, 52 BC

What did you find out?

1. Did these Roman writers have a high or a low opinion of the Britons? _____

2. Which phrase in source A shows what the writer thought of the Britons? _____
_____

3. Do any of these sources tell us what the Britons thought of the Romans? _____

4. What did the Romans hope that Caesar would find in Britain? _____
_____

5. In what order were the sources written? Write the answer in this space, with the earliest source first (write 'A', 'B' etc)._____

Primary and secondary sources

A primary source is a first-hand account, something written at the time of, or shortly after, the events described.

A secondary source is a second-hand account written later, based on earlier writings.

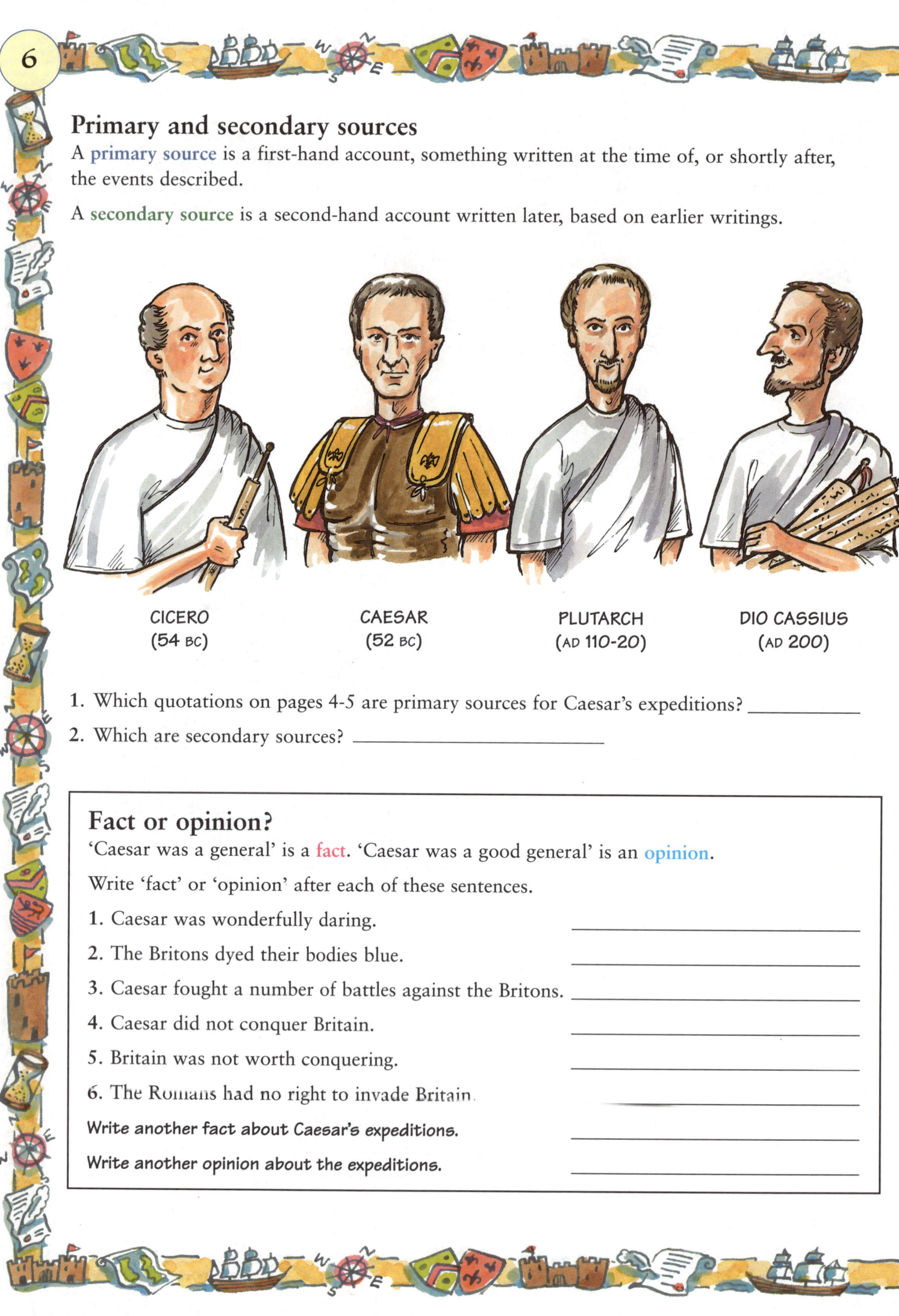

CICERO
(54 BC)

CAESAR
(52 BC)

PLUTARCH
(AD 110-20)

DIO CASSIUS
(AD 200)

1. Which quotations on pages 4-5 are primary sources for Caesar's expeditions? _____

2. Which are secondary sources? _____

Fact or opinion?

'Caesar was a general' is a fact. 'Caesar was a good general' is an opinion.

Write 'fact' or 'opinion' after each of these sentences.

1. Caesar was wonderfully daring.   _____

2. The Britons dyed their bodies blue.   _____

3. Caesar fought a number of battles against the Britons. _____

4. Caesar did not conquer Britain.   _____

5. Britain was not worth conquering.   _____

6. The Romans had no right to invade Britain.   _____

Write another fact about Caesar's expeditions.   _____

Write another opinion about the expeditions.   _____

Roman emperors

The Emperor Tiberius ruled Rome from AD 14-37. To find out what he was like, we depend on Roman historians. Unfortunately, they don't always agree with each other!

A historian called **Velleius Paterculus** knew Tiberius. While the emperor was still alive, Velleius described his rule:

A *'Who could list all the good things the emperor has done? His generosity benefits whole cities. He is the best of emperors, and he teaches his citizens to do right by doing it himself. Though he is greatest among us in power, he is even greater because of the good example he gives us!'*

A hundred years after Tiberius died, the emperor was described by another Roman historian, **Suetonius**:

B *'Tiberius was a tight-fisted miser. He did many wicked deeds because he liked seeing people suffer. He used to say, 'Let people hate me, so long as they fear me!'*

Some of these quotations about the Emperor Tiberius come from **Velleius**, and some from **Suetonius**. **Who wrote each one?**

1. 'In Capri, they still show the place at the cliff top where Tiberius used to watch his victims being thrown into the sea after lengthy tortures.'

   _____

2. 'What public buildings did he construct! With what pious generosity does he now build a temple to his father (Emperor Augustus)!'

   _____

3. 'No grand buildings marked his reign. His only two undertakings, the temple to Augustus and the restoration of Pompeii's theatre, were not finished.'

   _____

4. 'Let me end my book with a prayer. O Jupiter, Mars and Vesta, and all other gods who have watched over Rome, I call on you: protect the present state of things, the peace which we now enjoy, and our present Emperor Tiberius.'

   _____

FRANÇAIS (FRENCH)

The holiday game

Make a French colour dice (shown below), then play this game to practise some French phrases you might need on holiday. You must say the French phrase to stay on the square!

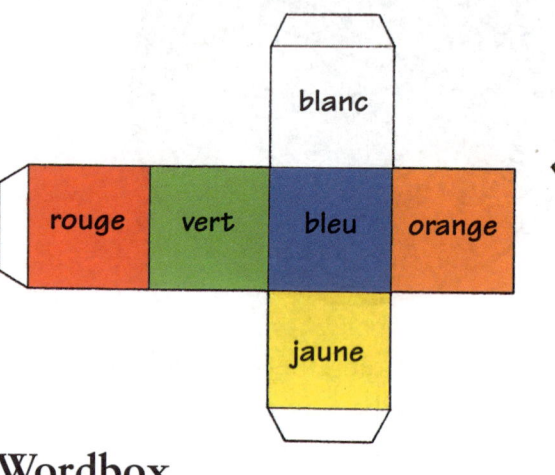

oui — yes

non — no

Top tips!

French pronunciation is tricky. Practise with these words and numbers:

1. Un — *un*
2. deux — *duh*
3. trois — *twa*
4. quatre — *katr*
5. cinq — *sank*
6. six — *seece*
7. sept — *set*
8. huit — *weet*
9. neuf — *nuf*
10. dix — *deece*

Wordbox

- Comment t'appelles-tu? – *What's your name?*
- Je m'appelle… – *My name is…*
- Ça va? – *How are you?*
- Tu as quel âge? – *How old are you?*
- Tu aimes… ? – *Do you like … ?*
- Comment dire… en Français? – *How do you say… in French?*
- S'il vous plaît – *Please*
- Merci – *Thank you*
- Salut – *Hello*
- Au revoir – *Goodbye*
- J'ai onze ans – *I'm eleven*
- Je ne comprends pas – *I do not understand*

ç – s

On parle Français (We speak French)

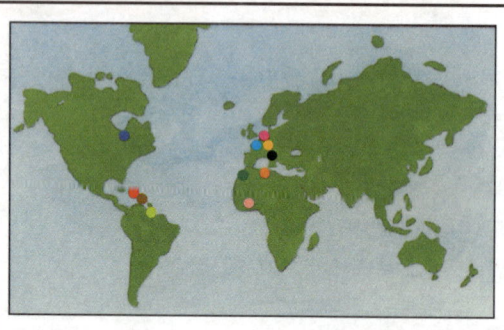

- France
- Belgique
- Luxembourg
- Suisse
- Maroc
- Algérie
- Afrique de l'ouest
- Québec
- Guadeloupe
- Martinique
- Guyane

Au revoir!

DIX-SEPT

DETECTIVE WORK

Would you make a good witness?

Look carefully at this picture for a minute and try to remember the details of what you see. After one minute, cover the picture and answer the questions without cheating!

1. How many robbers were there? _____

2. What was the name of the bank? _____

3. What colour was the car that had broken down? _____

4. What sort of van was being unloaded? _____

5. What was next to the bank? _____

6. How many people were sitting on the bench? _____

7. Did the bank have an alarm? _____

8. Were any people on bicycles? _____

9. Was there a railway line nearby? _____

10. What was the woman in a yellow jumper doing? _____

Score ☐ 10 – Excellent   ☐ 8–9 – Very good   ☐ 6–7 – Not bad
☐ 5 or under – You need to improve your powers of observation!

The break-in

Last night, as you were passing Lord Snoot's mansion, you saw a burglar.
You managed to take several photographs but they have got jumbled up. Number the photographs
in order. Write a sentence about each photograph to describe what you saw.

Witness Crime Report *Signed* _____

1. _____
2. _____
3. _____
4. _____
5. _____
6. _____
7. _____
8. _____

Remember to give lots of details. What details will help the police?

A secret code saves the day

2,000 years ago the Athenians and the Spartans, who came from different cities in Greece, were at war. Lysander, the Spartan general, was camped with his army a long way from Sparta. The citizens of Sparta needed to get an urgent message to him, but the problem was that he was surrounded by the Athenian army!

One day Lysander looked up to see a boy, dressed in a tunic and belt and wearing sandals, running into his camp. Lysander was amazed. 'I have a message from the people of Sparta,' the boy gasped.

'Weren't you stopped by the Athenians?' Lysander asked.

'Many times,' the boy replied, 'but they could not find anything so they let me go.'

Lysander smiled when he saw the boy's belt. It had a jumble of meaningless letters on it. Lysander took the belt and wound it round the pole of his javelin so that the edges of it touched. All at once a message could be seen. The message told him that the Persians, who had been their allies, had double-crossed him and joined with the Athenians.

Thanks to the cleverly coded message, Lysander was able to prepare his army to fight his new enemy.

Cracking the code

KEY

1	2	3	4	5	6	7	8	9	10	11	12	13	14	15	16	17	18	19	20	21	22	23	24	25	26
A	B	C	D	E	F	G	H	I	J	K	L	M	N	O	P	Q	R	S	T	U	V	W	X	Y	Z

Use the simple code above to 'crack' this message.

13	5	5	20
M	E	E	T

13	5

20	15	14	9	7	8	20

21	14	4	5	18

20	8	5

15	12	4

23	15	15	4	5	14

2	18	9	4	7	5

13	1	11	5

19	21	18	5

25	15	21

1	18	5

14	15	20

6	15	12	12	15	23	5	4

18	5	13	5	13	2	5	18

20	15

2	18	9	14	7

20	8	5

19	5	3	18	5	20

16	1	16	5	18	19

Now try a picture code:

KEY

A ⌐	G ⌐	M ▣	S ∨	Y ◁
B ⌐⌐	H ⊓	N ▣	T >	Z ⧊
C ⌐	I ⌐	O ▣	U <	
D ⌐	J ▪	P ▣	V ∧	
E □	K ▣	Q ▣	W ∨	
F ⌐	L ▪	R ▣	X ▷	

Work out what this message says using the key.

Make up some more messages in these codes, and send them to a friend.

_____

_____

_____

_____

_____

_____

_____

AT THE TRAVEL AGENT

Foreign travel

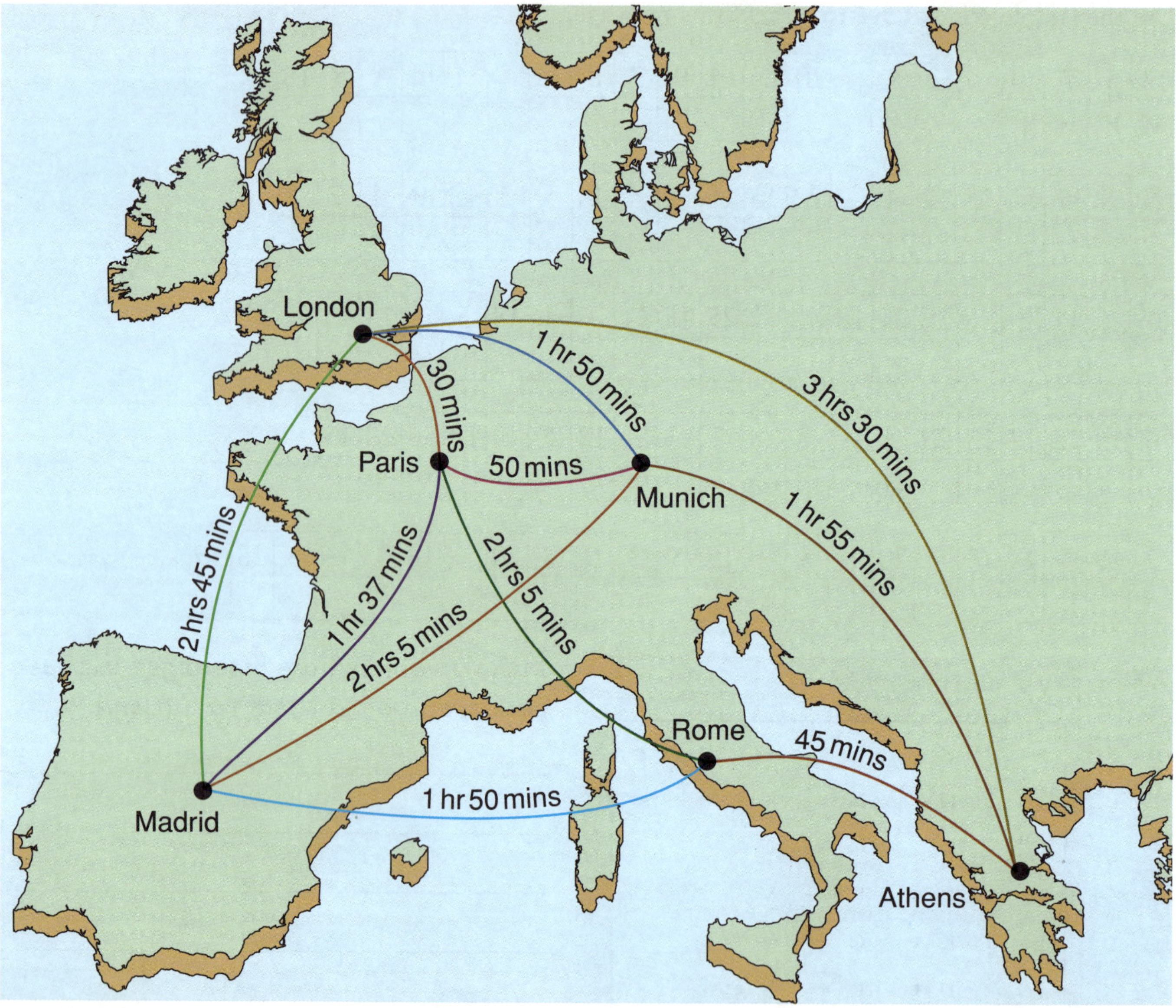

This map of western Europe shows some major cities and the time it takes to fly between them. It is not always possible to fly direct from one city to another. Sometimes you must go via another city, for example from Madrid to Athens via Rome.

The travel agent

Imagine you are a travel agent. Your job is to help people book flights to go to some of these cities. How would you answer the questions on the next page?

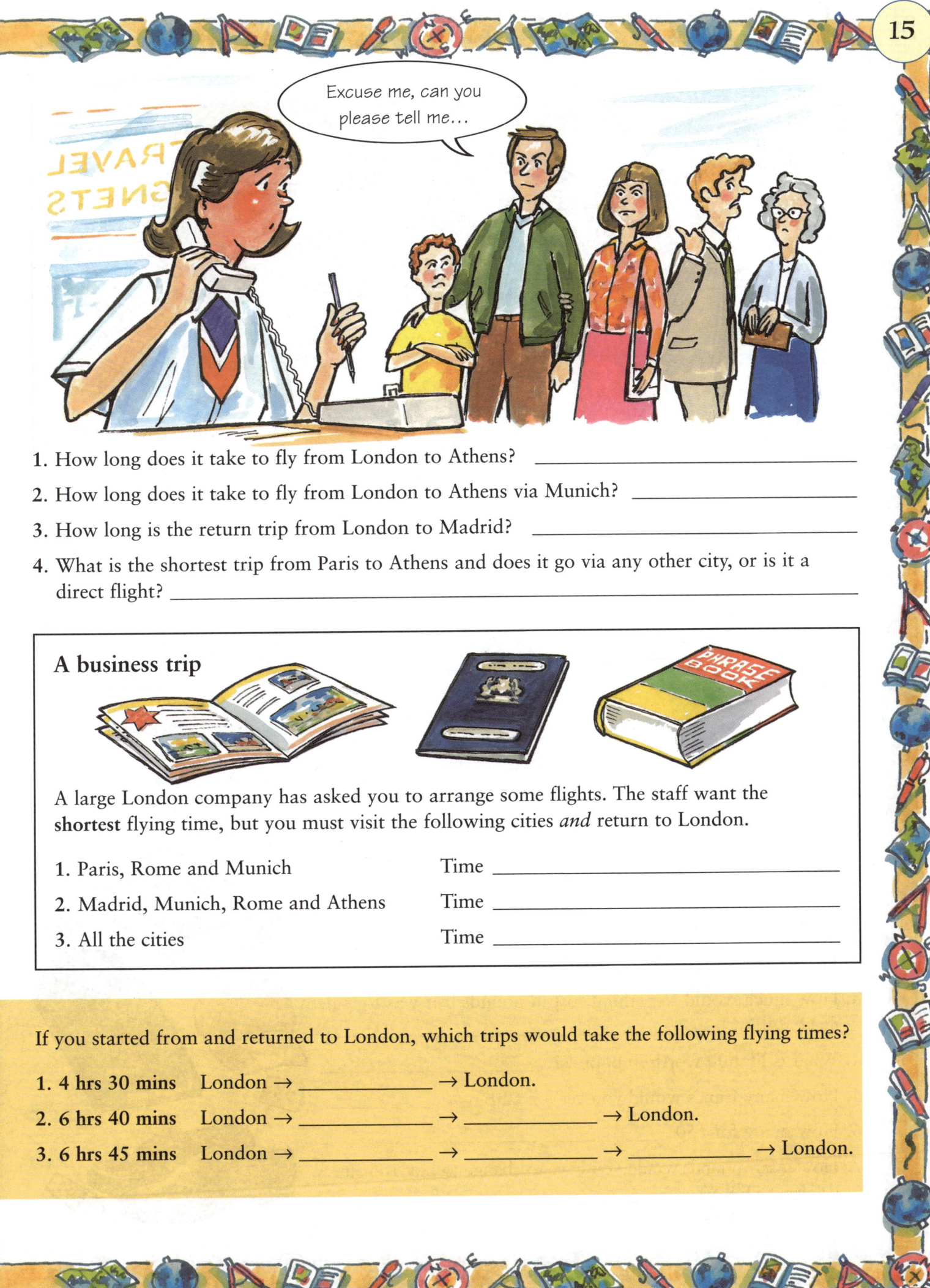

Excuse me, can you please tell me…

1. How long does it take to fly from London to Athens? _____

2. How long does it take to fly from London to Athens via Munich? _____

3. How long is the return trip from London to Madrid? _____

4. What is the shortest trip from Paris to Athens and does it go via any other city, or is it a direct flight? _____

A business trip

A large London company has asked you to arrange some flights. The staff want the **shortest** flying time, but you must visit the following cities *and* return to London.

1. Paris, Rome and Munich   Time _____

2. Madrid, Munich, Rome and Athens   Time _____

3. All the cities   Time _____

If you started from and returned to London, which trips would take the following flying times?

1. **4 hrs 30 mins**   London → _____ → London.

2. **6 hrs 40 mins**   London → _____ → _____ → London.

3. **6 hrs 45 mins**   London → _____ → _____ → _____ → London.

Foreign exchange

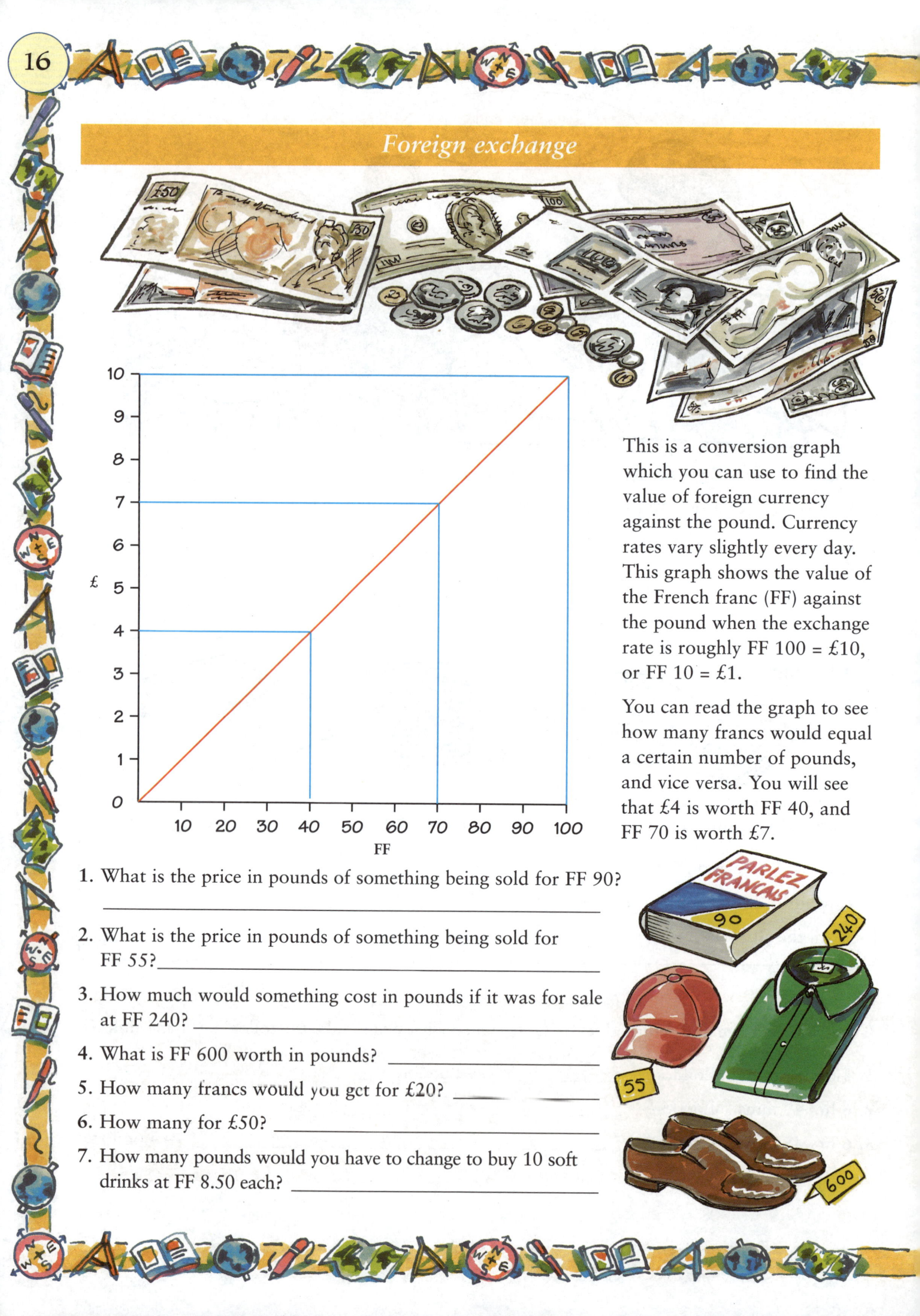

This is a conversion graph which you can use to find the value of foreign currency against the pound. Currency rates vary slightly every day. This graph shows the value of the French franc (FF) against the pound when the exchange rate is roughly FF 100 = £10, or FF 10 = £1.

You can read the graph to see how many francs would equal a certain number of pounds, and vice versa. You will see that £4 is worth FF 40, and FF 70 is worth £7.

1. What is the price in pounds of something being sold for FF 90?
   _____

2. What is the price in pounds of something being sold for FF 55? _____

3. How much would something cost in pounds if it was for sale at FF 240? _____

4. What is FF 600 worth in pounds? _____

5. How many francs would you get for £20? _____

6. How many for £50? _____

7. How many pounds would you have to change to buy 10 soft drinks at FF 8.50 each? _____

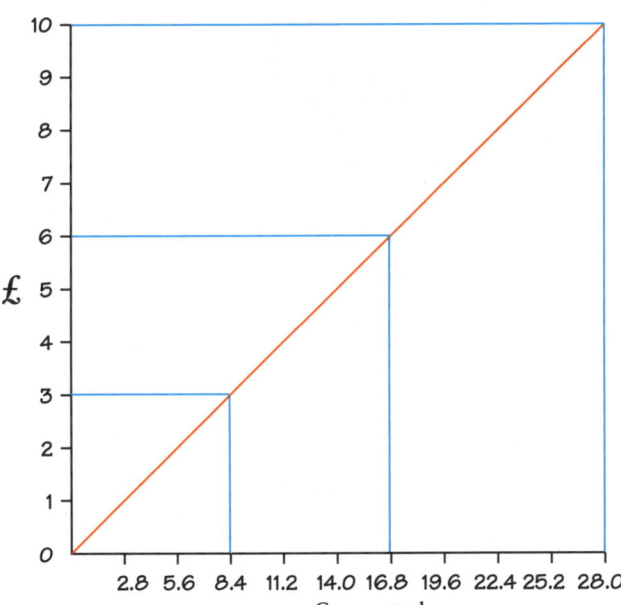

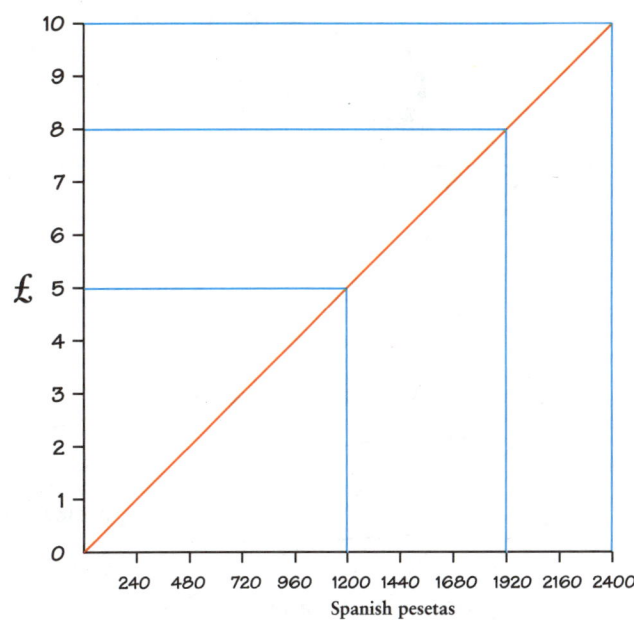

German marks

Here is a conversion graph for German marks (DM) against the pound, at an exchange rate of DM 2.8 = £1. You can see that £3 = DM 8.4.

1. What is the price in pounds of something at DM 22.4? _____

2. How many marks would you get for £7?

_____

Spanish pesetas

Here is a conversion graph for Spanish pesetas against the pound, at an exchange rate of 240 pesetas = £1.

You can see that £5 = 1200 pesetas.

1. What is the price in pounds of something at 1440 pesetas? _____

2. How many pesetas would you get for £8?

_____

Approximation

The easiest way to convert money is by **approximation**, for example:

a. You have £15 to convert at £1 = DM 2.8.

b. Round this up so that £1 = DM 3.

c. 15 x 3 = £45.

You know that you will get a little less than £45.00.

Round these figures up or down so that they are easier to multiply.

£1 = FF 8.9   £1 = FF _____   so £12 = FF _____   £1 = $1.6   £1 = $ _____   so £16 = $ _____

£1 = 240 pesetas   £1 = _____ pesetas   so £9 = _____ pesetas

Use a calculator

You can also work out your foreign exchange on a calculator.

If £1 = DM 2.8, for example, then to find how many marks you would pay for something, just **multiply** the price in pounds by 2.8. So £15 = 15 x 2.8 = DM 42.

To find how much something costs in pounds, just **divide** the price by 2.8.
So a T-shirt at DM 21 would cost £7.50.

OUR LANGUAGE

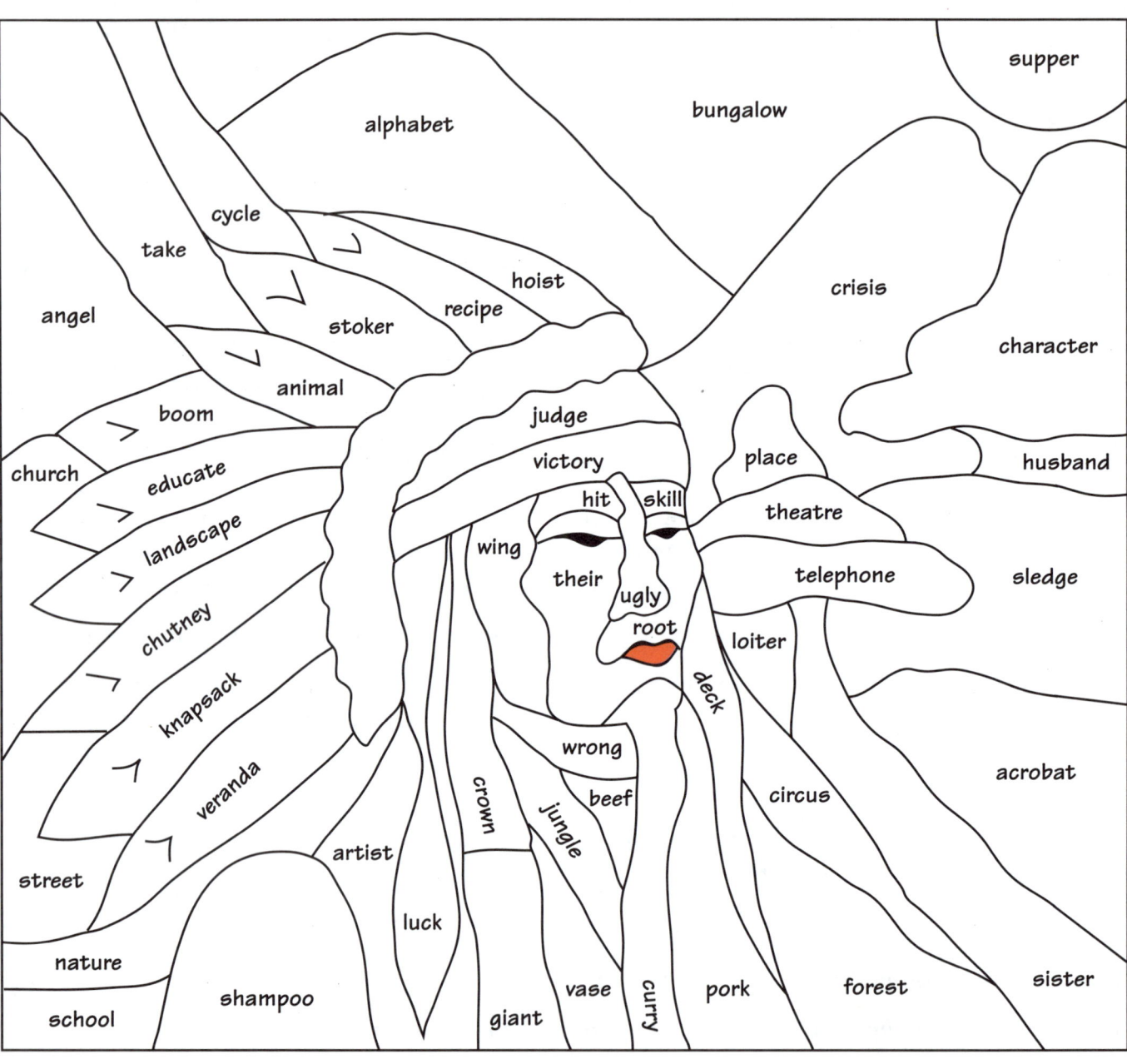

Find the words in this picture.

Check them in the boxes on the next page. Colour them in to discover the hidden secret.

Use the colour key to help you colour them in.

- ■ Scandinavian words
- ■ Dutch words
- ■ French words
- ■ Greek words
- ■ Latin words
- ■ Indian words

Word origins

We call our language 'English' but it has been influenced by the languages of many other countries over the years. Here are a few of these influences.

Scandinavian

When the Vikings invaded 1,200 years ago they introduced words such as:

wrong	take
sister	husband
skill	hit
ugly	their
wing	root

Dutch

We have had trading links with the Dutch for centuries. We have 'borrowed' words like these from them:

knapsack	stoker
landscape	sledge
luck	loiter
boom	deck
hoist	

French

The Normans invaded from France in 1066 and introduced words such as:

beef	nature
vase	artist
forest	supper
pork	judge

Greek

The ancient Greek civilisation contributed many words to English:

crisis	angel
cycle	place
theatre	church
alphabet	telephone
character	acrobat

Latin

The Romans brought Latin words, which are used in many languages:

giant	victory
educate	animal
school	street
circus	crown
recipe	

Indian

During the 19th century, many words from India entered our language:

curry	chutney
bungalow	jungle
veranda	shampoo

Days of the week

The ancient Romans chose seven days as the length of a week, naming them after the seven bright objects they could see in the sky, which were also the names of gods. The Anglo-Saxons in England changed these into their own gods.

Roman beginning	Anglo-Saxon god	Day
Sol (sun god)	Sunna	Sunday
Luna (moon goddess)	Mona	Monday
Mars (god of war)	Tiw	Tuesday
Mercury (god of learning and magic)	Woden	Wednesday
Jupiter (sky god)	Thunor	Thursday
Venus (goddess of love)	Frigg	Friday
Saturn (god of farming)	Saetern	Saturday

English spelling

Words are not always what they seem! Take care when you read this poem.

I take it you already know
Of tough and bough and cough and dough?
Others may stumble, but not you
On hiccough, thorough, laugh and through?
Well done! And now you wish perhaps
To learn of less familiar traps?

Beware of heard, a dreadful word
That looks like beard and sounds like bird.
And dead: it's said like bed, not bead –
For goodness sake don't call it deed!
Watch out for meat and great and threat,
They rhyme with suite and straight and debt.

Crossword

Use some of the words in the poem to complete the crossword.

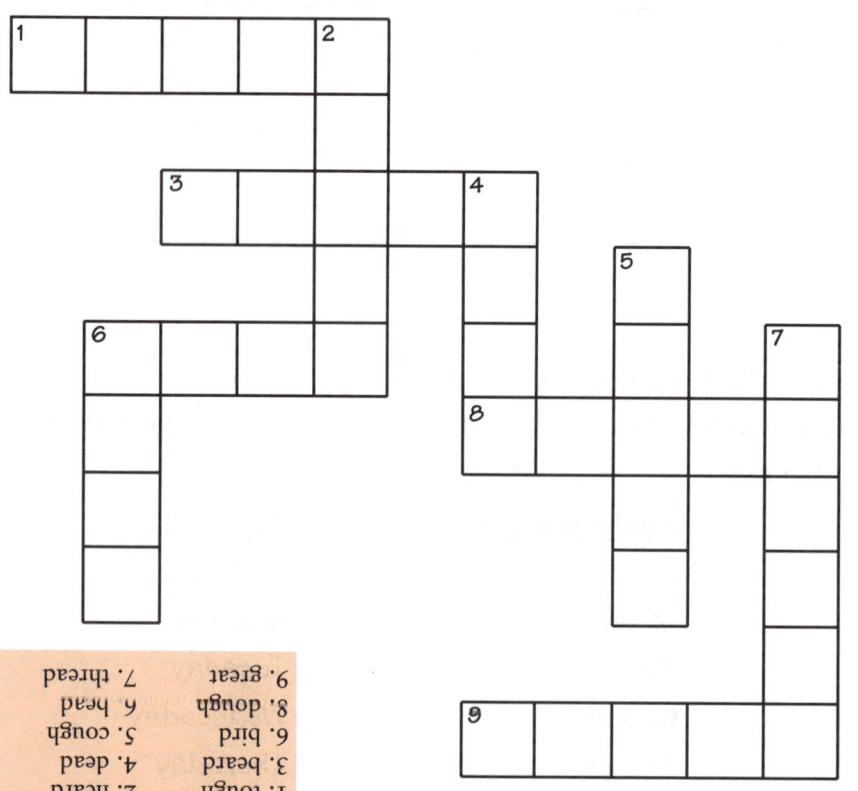

Clues across

1. Strong, or hard to chew.

3. Hair growing on a man's face.

6. An animal with feathers, wings and a beak.

8. Used for making bread.

9. Large or important.

Clues down

2. This word contains ear.

4. Not alive.

5. To make a sudden loud noise in your throat.

6. You use lots of these to make a necklace.

7. A promise to do something bad.

Answers
Across
1. tough 2. heard
3. beard 4. dead
6. bird   5. cough
8. dough 6. bead
9. great 7. thread
Down

Test your vocabulary

Put a circle around T or F to show if the following statements are true or false.
You may need a dictionary to help you.

1. You can eat **tapioca**.   T   F
2. A **cacophony** is a prickly plant.   T   F
3. A **physician** is a doctor.   T   F
4. A **dormitory** is where mice live.   T   F
5. You can get lost in a **maize**.   T   F
6. If something is **rancid** it tastes horrible.   T   F
7. A **philatelist** collects coins.   T   F
8. A **rickshaw** is a kind of boat.   T   F
9. A **hostile** person is unfriendly.   T   F
10. If you are **raucous** you are a quiet person.   T   F
11. **Stationery** is something you write on.   T   F
12. A **cereal** is a story told in episodes.   T   F
13. An **umpire** is a kind of referee.   T   F
14. A **muscle** is a kind of shellfish.   T   F

Choose the right word

A Cross out the wrong word in each sentence:

1. The bicycle was for (sail/sale).
2. The (hole/whole) pizza was ruined.
3. The (pane/pain) of glass was broken.
4. We walked on the golf (coarse/course).
5. A (horde/hoard) of children came rushing towards me.

B Insert the words in the correct places:

1. (allowed/aloud) We are not _____ to speak _____ in class.
2. (scent/sent)   My gran did not like the _____ I _____ her.
3. (stair/stare) I saw him _____ at the man on the _____.
4. (piece/peace) You will get no _____ until you give him a _____ of cake.
5. (bored/board) The _____ builder nailed up the _____.

EUROPEAN TOUR

Spot it on the map

Look at this map of Europe and the flags below.

1. Write the names of the countries on the map.

2. Write in the names of the capital cities marked in red on the map.

3. Try to name the rest of the countries.

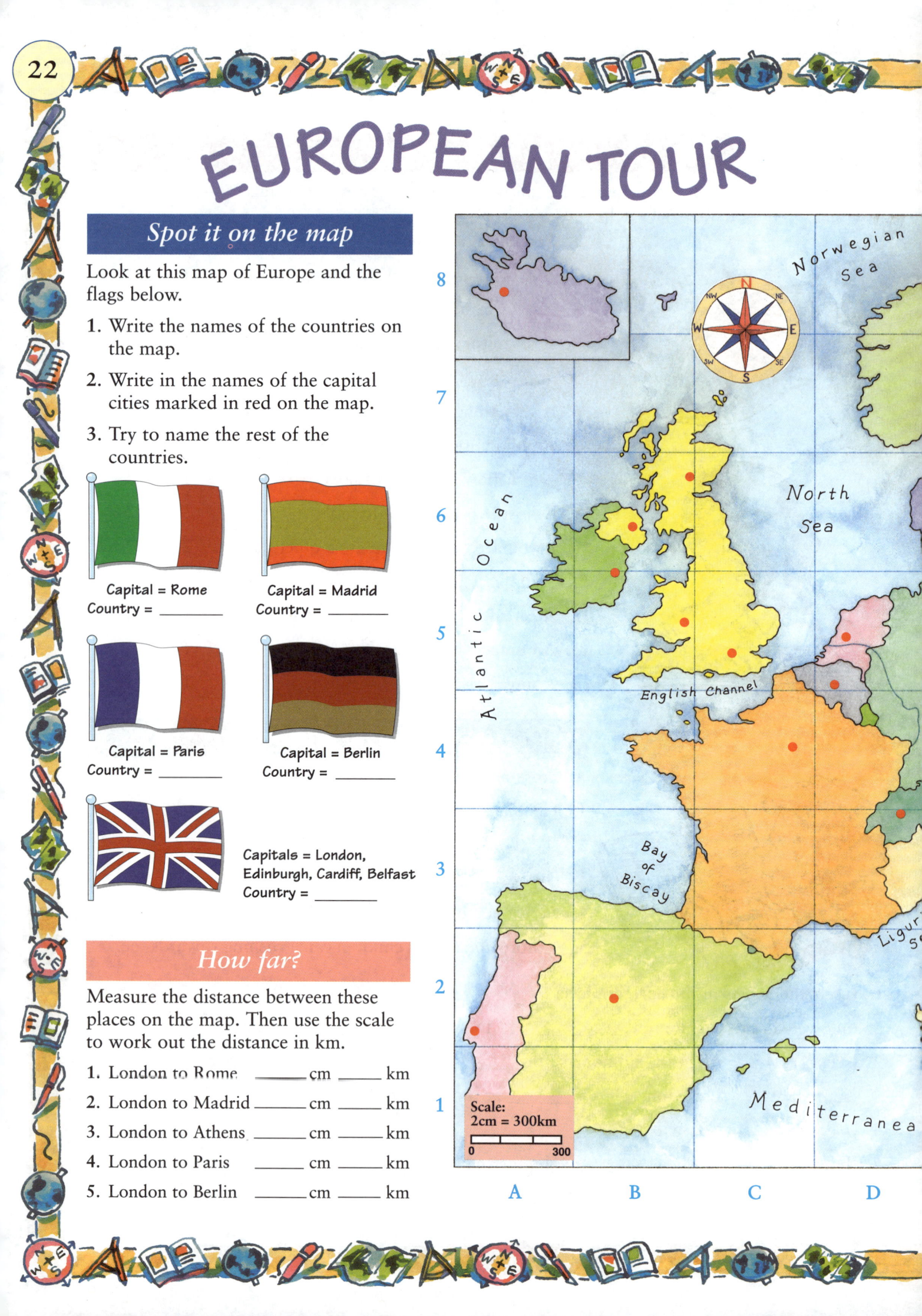

Capital = Rome
Country = _____

Capital = Madrid
Country = _____

Capital = Paris
Country = _____

Capital = Berlin
Country = _____

Capitals = London,
Edinburgh, Cardiff, Belfast
Country = _____

How far?

Measure the distance between these places on the map. Then use the scale to work out the distance in km.

1. London to Rome _____ cm _____ km

2. London to Madrid _____ cm _____ km

3. London to Athens _____ cm _____ km

4. London to Paris _____ cm _____ km

5. London to Berlin _____ cm _____ km

Norwegian Sea

North Sea

Atlantic Ocean

English Channel

Bay of Biscay

Ligurian Se

Mediterranea

Scale:
2cm = 300km

0   300

8

7

6

5

4

3

2

1

A   B   C   D

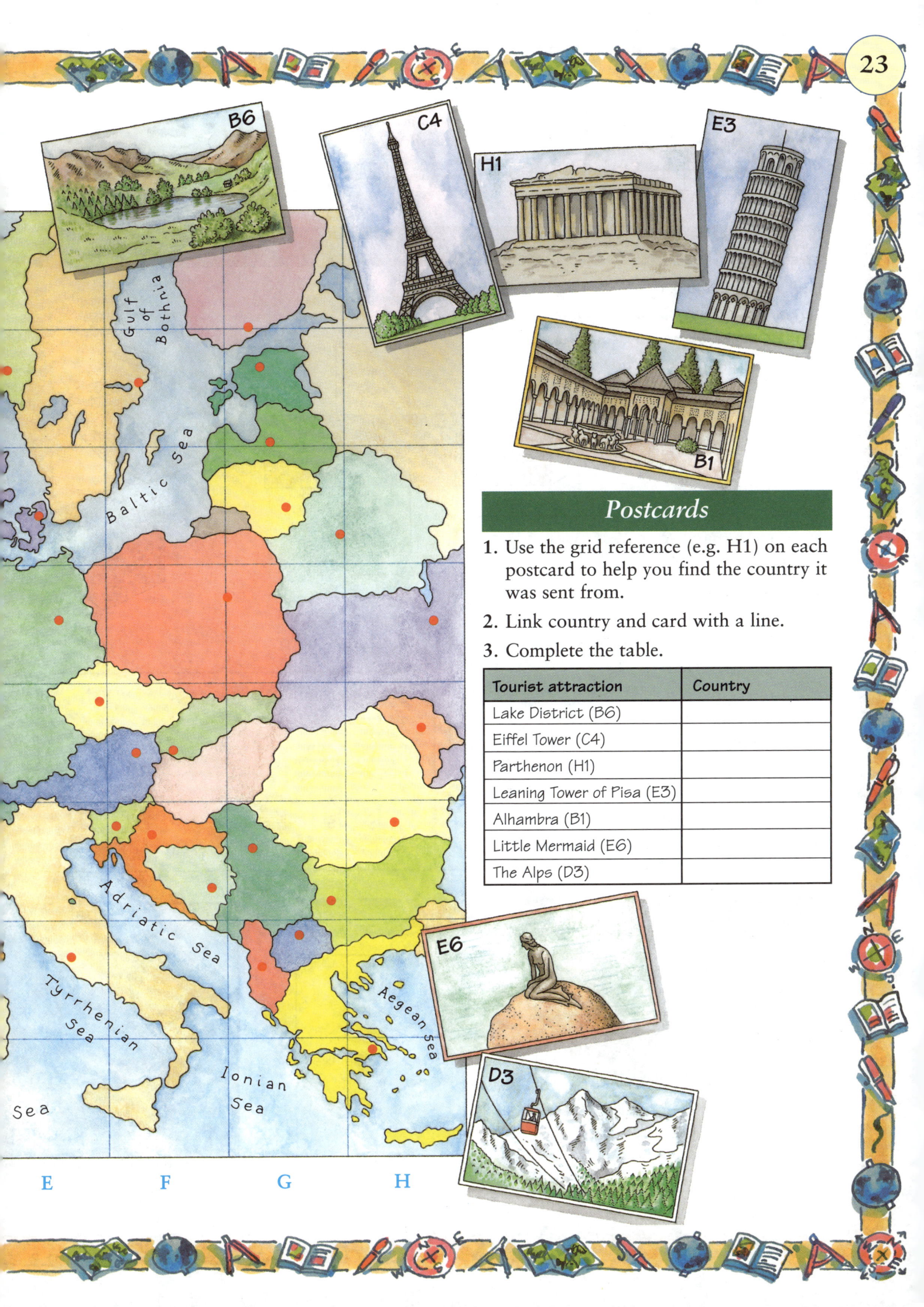

Postcards

1. Use the grid reference (e.g. H1) on each postcard to help you find the country it was sent from.

2. Link country and card with a line.

3. Complete the table.

Tourist attraction	Country
Lake District (B6)	
Eiffel Tower (C4)	
Parthenon (H1)	
Leaning Tower of Pisa (E3)	
Alhambra (B1)	
Little Mermaid (E6)	
The Alps (D3)	

ESPAÑOL (SPANISH)

The holiday game

Make a Spanish dice (shown below), then play this game to practise some Spanish phrases you might need on holiday. You must say the Spanish phrase to stay on the square!

		2 dos		
6 seis	5 cinco	3 tres	1 uno	
		4 cuatro		

Wordbox

- ¿Cómo te llamas? – *What's your name?*
- Me llamo… – *My name is…*
- ¿Qué tal? – *How are you?*
- ¿Cuantos años tienes? – *How old are you?*
- Tengo once años – *I'm eleven*
- ¿Te gusta? – *Do you like… ?*
- ¿Cómo se dice en español? – *How do you say… in Spanish?*
- Por favor – *Please*
- Gracias – *Thank you*
- ¡Hola! – *Hello*
- ¡Adios! – *Goodbye*
- No entiendo – *I don't understand*

Top tips!

Spanish pronunciation is easy, but watch out for these:

ll = pronounced '*y*' as in 'yacht'
'me llamo' = 'may yamo'

c = followed by a vowel = '*th*' as in 'three'
e.g. 'gracias' = 'grathias'

ñ = '*ny*' e.g. 'español' = 'espanyol'

¿Dónde se habla español? (We speak Spanish)

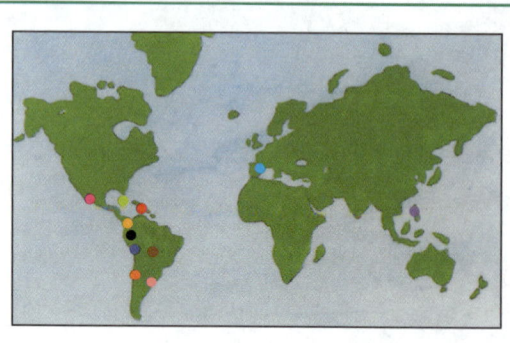

- España
- México
- Colombia
- Ecuador
- Perú
- Cuba
- Chile
- Argentina
- Puerto Rico
- Las Filipinas
- Bolivia

¡Adios!

17

DIECISIETE

25

 # SARAH

I suppose I was jealous. We all were, at first. That Sarah – she seemed to have everything. Her family had just moved into the huge stone house in Rookery Road – the one with the enormous garden and the tennis court. My Mum used to call it Buckingham Palace! Sarah had her own TV, her own phone and her own bathroom. She even had her own pony, for goodness' sake! My brother Jack and I used to see her riding past, with her nose up in the air. Or so we thought, at the time.

We live in an ordinary house, with one ordinary bathroom whose cold tap won't stop dripping, and a titchy little garden where Jack keeps a couple of rabbits and a hamster. Not much chance of getting a pony in there! I share a bedroom with my sister Rachel, and we all have endless fights about who's going to use the bathroom next, and what we're going to watch on TV. Mum and Dad usually have the last word, but Mum doesn't really mind – as long as she doesn't miss her favourite soaps, that is.

We didn't use to talk to Sarah very much. We thought she was stuck up, and anyway, it was depressing to watch her parading all her expensive things. Clothes, tapes, sports gear – you name it, she had it. Always the latest stuff, too. Nobody liked to ask her how much pocket money she got.

When we did talk to her, it was in a nasty way – you know, trying to put her down. Once she came to school wearing a new jacket that I'd been looking at every day in the shop window. I was saving up for it, though I knew it would take me about a million years to get enough money. When Sarah asked me if I liked it, I just pulled a face and said that nobody was wearing those any more, were they?

At school, last term, we were doing projects about ourselves and our lives – our families, our friends, what we did in our free time, what we wanted to be when we grew up – that sort of thing. One playtime, as we were filing out of the classroom, I saw that Sarah had left her project on her table. I decided to sneak a look at it. I thought it would be full of showing off and boasting about all her things – I'd be able to tell the others and we could all have a good laugh.

There was another time, when Sarah asked Jack if he'd like to borrow a computer game, and he said he'd got it already, thanks very much. He hadn't really, of course.

I know it wasn't very nice of us, but we couldn't help it. It just didn't seem fair.

Things are different now, though. Sarah and I are best friends, and I often go to the house in Rookery Road at the weekends. Sometimes we go shopping together, or we listen to CDs. She's really great, Sarah. Something happened, you see – something that changed the way I felt about her, for good.

I pretended to be looking for something in my locker, and when the room was empty I picked up Sarah's notebook and looked inside. This is what I read.

'My name is Sarah. I'm eleven years old and I live in London. There are just three of us in my family – Mum, Dad and me – but I've got a dog called Sandy and a pony called Firefly.

'My hobbies are reading (mystery stories), and playing computer games. If the weather is good I go riding or take Sandy for a walk.

'At school, I like most subjects, really, except games. Nobody ever seems to pick me to be in their team. I don't seem to be much good at making friends. I'm a bit shy, and it's hard to have to start a new school where everyone knows each other…'

That was as far as she'd got.

I stood there for a long time, the book dangling from my hand. Sarah's project seemed to be all about the things she *didn't* have. There was nothing about brothers and sisters, nothing about things she did with her Mum and Dad. All her hobbies were things you could do on your own – there was nothing about friends, apart from the fact that she didn't really have any. And as for the fantastic house, the clothes, the vast amounts of pocket money – they weren't mentioned at all. Mystery stories, though – *I* liked those, too…

I put the project back where I'd found it, and walked thoughtfully out of the classroom.

The next day was Friday, so the first lesson was games. We all trooped on to the school field with the rounders equipment, and I asked if I could pick one of the teams. I looked slowly round at all the faces, but I knew who I was going to choose first…

After school, Rachel met me at the gates.

'I'm glad that day's over,' she grumbled. 'You wouldn't believe how hard that new teacher makes us work! Oh, no – there's Sarah! I bet she wants to walk to the bus stop with us. I'm not in the mood to listen to her going on about her precious pony. Come on, let's hide!'

She dived behind a bush, dragging a bag full of homework behind her.

'Actually,' I said slowly, 'Sarah's not as bad as all that, not when you get to know her. She's asked me to go round to her house tomorrow – well, I wouldn't mind having a ride on her pony. His name's Firefly. She's all right, Sarah. Oh, yes, and she's really good at rounders.'

Sarah had caught up with us by this time.

'Hi, Sarah,' I said. 'Do you want to walk to the bus stop with us? Rachel's just, er…'

Rachel emerged from behind the bush, picking leaves out of her hair.

'I was just looking for my crisps,' she said. 'They, er, fell out of my bag. It's stuffed full of homework… Do you want some, Sarah?'

LONDON'S BURNING

During the early hours of Sunday 2 September 1666, a fire broke out in a baker's shop at Pudding Lane in London. By morning, the flames had spread to many of the surrounding houses. Fanned by a strong wind, the fire was soon out of control. The flames raged for more than three days, destroying most of the city of London.

How the fire spread

This map shows the spread of the fire from Sunday until Wednesday morning, when it died out. X marks the spot where the fire started.

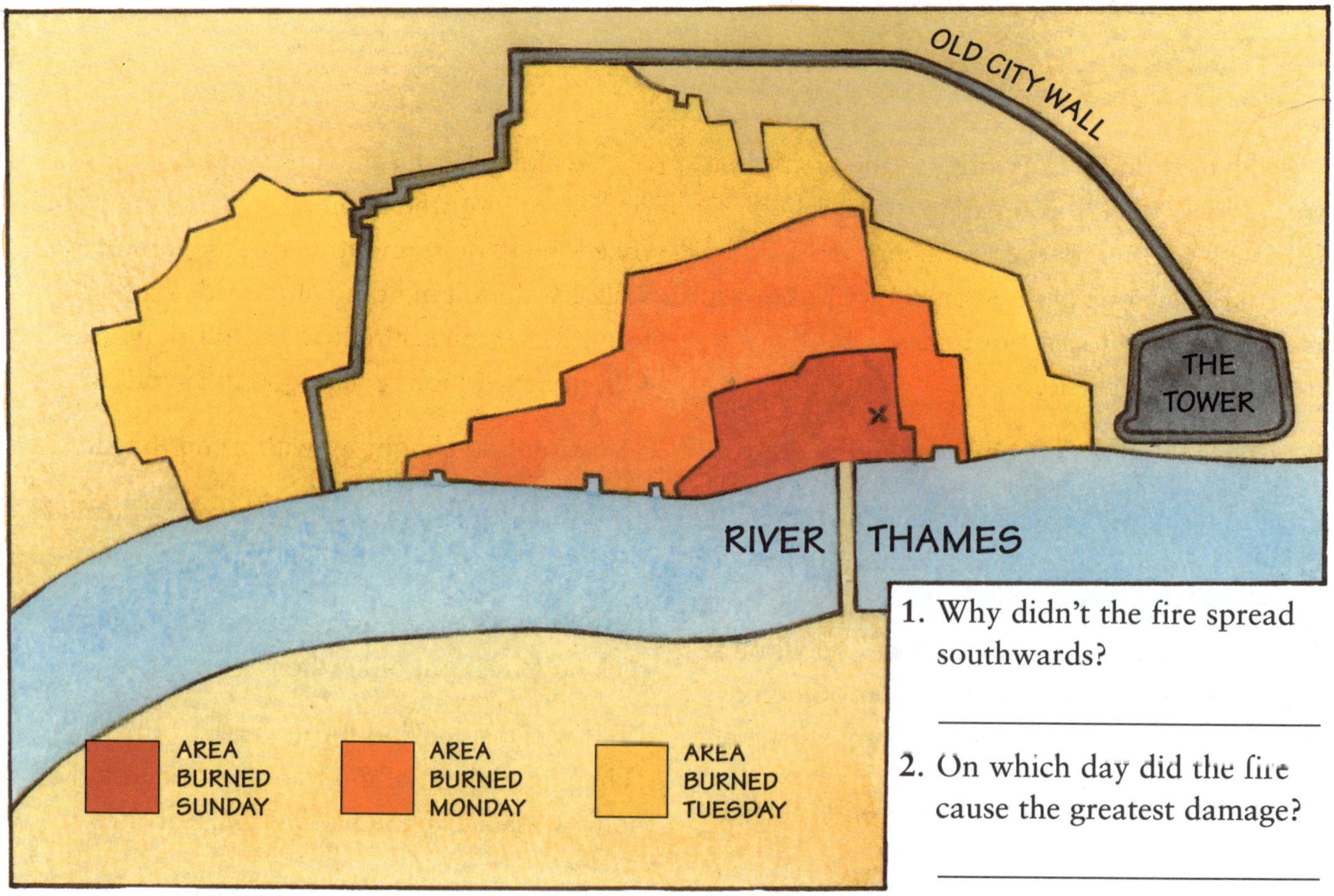

OLD CITY WALL

THE TOWER

RIVER THAMES

AREA BURNED SUNDAY

AREA BURNED MONDAY

AREA BURNED TUESDAY

1. Why didn't the fire spread southwards?

_____

2. On which day did the fire cause the greatest damage?

_____

Samuel Pepys was an important government official. On Sunday evening, he watched the fire from an alehouse on the south bank of the River Thames:

'We stayed till, it being darkish, we saw the fire as only one entire arch of fire. It made me weep to see it. The churches, houses and all on fire and flaming at once, and a horrid noise the flames made, and the cracking of houses at their ruin.'

Samuel Pepys, Diary.

Which words in this quotation tell you how Pepys felt about the fire?

Why did London burn?

This is part of a view of London drawn in the 1640s. It shows the area by the river where the fire first took hold. Look at the picture closely. Can you see why there was a risk of fire?

You can see that the houses and warehouses were built very closely together. Most of these buildings were wooden, and the warehouses held hay, timber, oil, tar, and other materials which burn easily. The long, hot summer of 1666 added to the fire risks. There was a water shortage, and the wooden buildings, dried out by the hot sun, were ready to burn.

Now draw your own picture of this part of London on fire.

Fighting the fire

There were no fire brigades in the 1600s. When a fire broke out, everyone was expected to work together to put it out. Fire-fighting equipment included leather buckets, ladders, fire-hooks and hand-squirts.

This is a fire-hook. It was used to pull down a building to make a **fire-break** – a space to stop the fire spreading. Fire-breaks could also be made by blowing up a building with gunpowder.

This is a brass hand-squirt, which worked like a bicycle pump. Two men held the handles while a third squirted water at the fire.

This 1613 print shows a fire which destroyed much of the town of Tiverton in Devon.

1. Which fire-fighting method is used by the people marked 'A'? _____

2. What are the people marked 'B' doing? _____

3. Why have the people at 'B' chosen this particular building? _____

4. What are the people marked 'C' doing? _____

5. Which seventeenth-century fire-fighting methods are not shown in the picture? _____

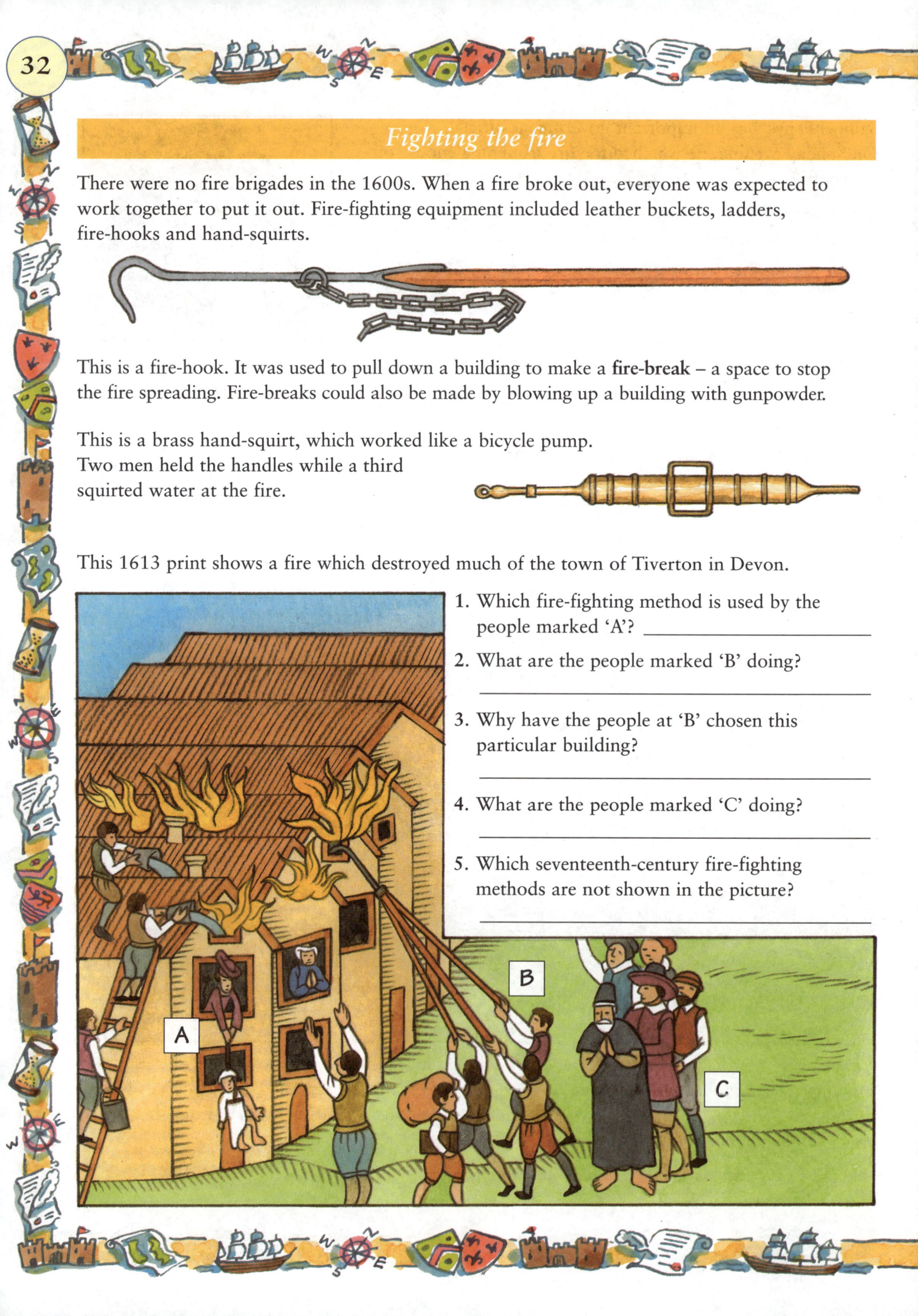

An accident... or a punishment?

This wooden statue *(right)* was put up on the wall of a tavern, marking the point where the fire ended. The inscription says that the fire was caused by 'the sin of gluttony', or greed for food. This idea came from a preacher, who pointed out that the fire 'began in Pudding Lane and ended at Pie Corner'.

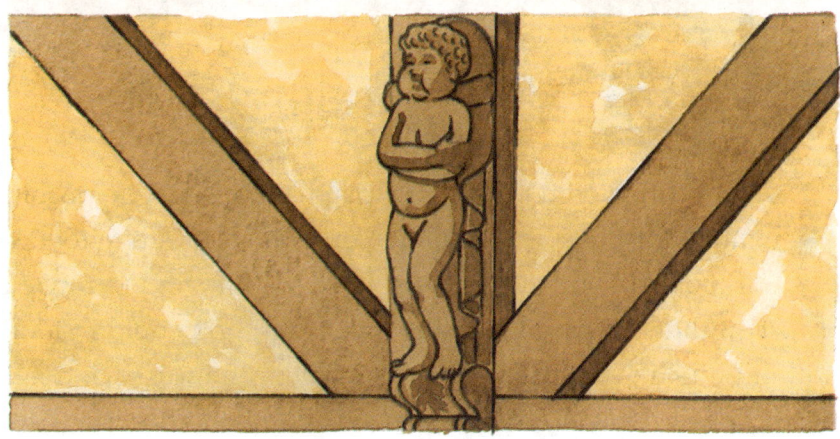

A Catholic explanation

England was a Protestant country. An account printed in Spain, a Catholic country, claimed that the fire had spared just one church – a Catholic one:

'May God open their eyes to the truth, and make them learn a lesson from the destruction of their own hundred and forty churches and the safety of the one Roman Catholic church, the only building that the flames respected.'

A New and True Account of the Formidable Fire, 1666

What lesson did this writer hope that the English would learn from the fire?

_____

A Dutch account

The Dutch, who were at war with England, printed their own account of the fire:

'Men, women and children ran through the streets, making a heart rending murmur. But in all their terrible suffering, not one person turned to Heaven to ask for mercy. They only cursed their fate and grew more cruel. The greatest crimes were committed, particularly against the large numbers of foreigners who lived in London, many of whom were murdered.'

Dutch account of the fire printed in Italy, 1666

1. Does this account have a bias **in favour of** or **against** the English? _____

2. Which part of the account makes you think that it might not be true? _____

_____

Find out more about the fire

You can research the Great Fire in your library. If possible, visit the Museum of London to learn more. How was the city rebuilt after the fire? Was London a safer place to live?

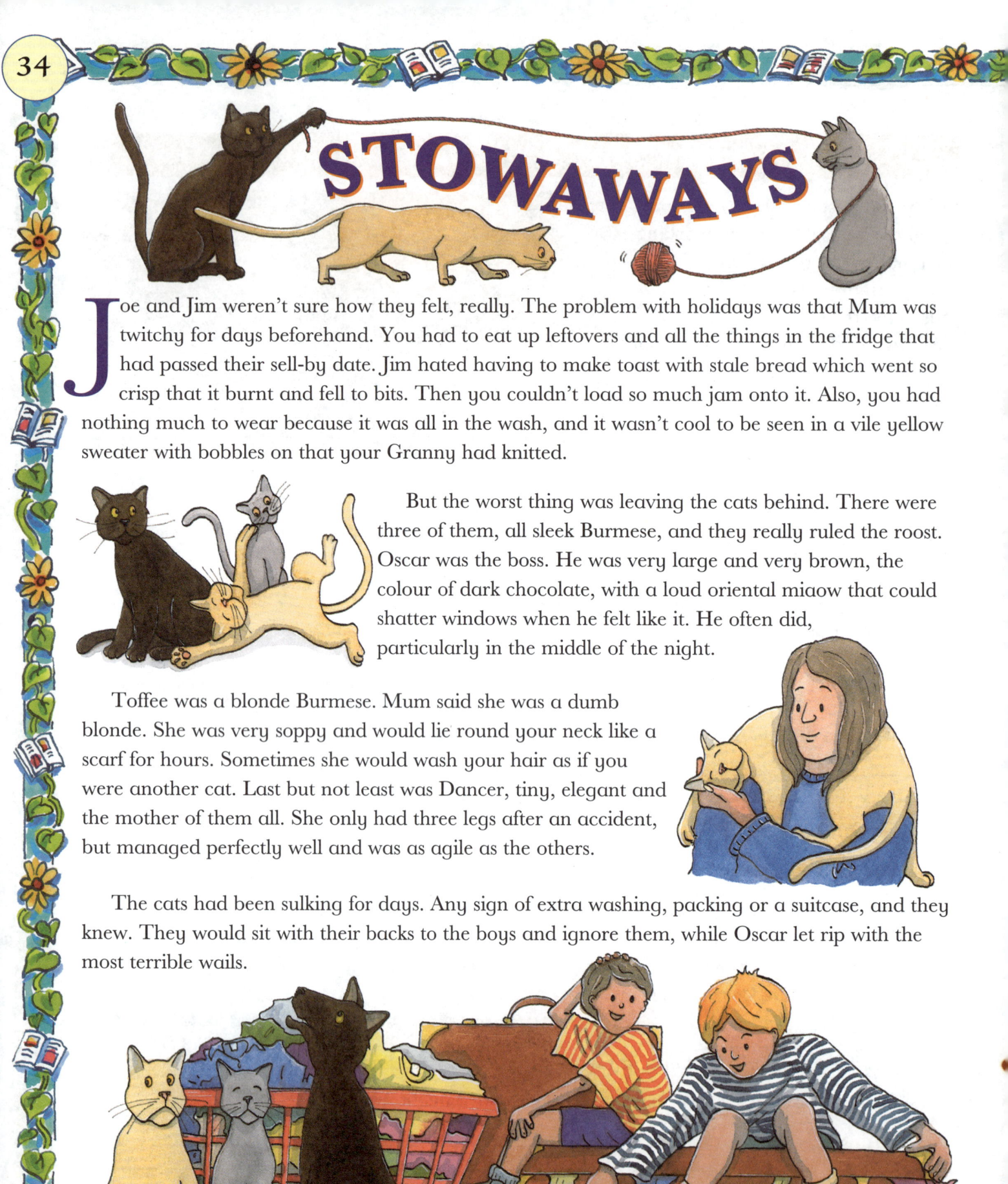

STOWAWAYS

Joe and Jim weren't sure how they felt, really. The problem with holidays was that Mum was twitchy for days beforehand. You had to eat up leftovers and all the things in the fridge that had passed their sell-by date. Jim hated having to make toast with stale bread which went so crisp that it burnt and fell to bits. Then you couldn't load so much jam onto it. Also, you had nothing much to wear because it was all in the wash, and it wasn't cool to be seen in a vile yellow sweater with bobbles on that your Granny had knitted.

But the worst thing was leaving the cats behind. There were three of them, all sleek Burmese, and they really ruled the roost. Oscar was the boss. He was very large and very brown, the colour of dark chocolate, with a loud oriental miaow that could shatter windows when he felt like it. He often did, particularly in the middle of the night.

Toffee was a blonde Burmese. Mum said she was a dumb blonde. She was very soppy and would lie round your neck like a scarf for hours. Sometimes she would wash your hair as if you were another cat. Last but not least was Dancer, tiny, elegant and the mother of them all. She only had three legs after an accident, but managed perfectly well and was as agile as the others.

The cats had been sulking for days. Any sign of extra washing, packing or a suitcase, and they knew. They would sit with their backs to the boys and ignore them, while Oscar let rip with the most terrible wails.

'Mary next door will feed them,' said Mum. 'They'll be perfectly all right. Help me to pack the car and sort out the caravan. Take these sheets into the caravan, boys, and help me to make the beds. We must stow all that food in the cupboards, too. Put the milk in the fridge.'

Eventually they were ready to go. The caravan was hitched up and Mum got into the car. 'Right, boys,' she said, 'Give those beasts a hug and shut them in the house.' 'I've done it already, Mum,' said Joe.

There was nothing else for it. The boys climbed into the car.

It was a long way to the campsite. They couldn't go fast with the caravan on the back and it was hot and sticky. Joe kept saying, 'How much further is it?' in a whiny sort of voice, and Jim kept saying, 'When are we going to get there?' They knew it would wind their mother up. Sure enough, the back of her neck and her ears got red and she crashed the gears so that the caravan swung behind them. They thought they'd better shut up or they wouldn't get there at all.

Then they started to feel excited. They had their first glimpse of the sea and drove down deep, steep lanes. 'What will we do if we meet another car, Mum?' asked Joe. 'Pray that we don't,' she said. 'I can't reverse the caravan.' Fortunately they reached the site without meeting anything.

They were welcomed by the farmer's wife who remembered them from last year. 'Hullo, boys,' she said. 'Help your mum set up the van over there by those trees. Some friends from last summer have been asking for you.'

Jim and Joe were keen to go and play with their old gang, but first they had to help unhitch the van. 'As it's nearly supper time we'll have a barbecue,' said Mum. 'Everybody else seems to be doing that. You get the little barbecue out of the boot and I'll get the food out of the fridge.' With that she opened the caravan door and let out a shriek. But there was second shriek, a miaowing, howling yowl of a shriek from Oscar, who rushed past at high speed followed by Dancer and Toffee, pieces of chicken dangling from their mouths.

'Those blasted cats!' said Mum, 'They've spent the whole journey raiding the fridge. They work as a team. Oscar's the ringleader! They've had the milk, the mince for tomorrow, some cheese and the cold chicken for our sandwiches, not to mention a carton of cream that I bought to have on the strawberries. And Oscar's eaten a hole in the fruit cake. I know it's him as he's the only one with a sweet tooth. Remember when he ate a hole in the caramel pudding before Granny came? I had to tidy it up neatly with a spoon and cut out the bits he'd touched and fill the hole with fruit. What she didn't know didn't hurt her. After them! I'll show them who's boss! How did they get in there, anyway?'

Joe and Jim exchanged a quick grin and shot off across the field, but there was no sign of the terrible trio.

'Oh, well, said Mum. 'I suppose it has its funny side. They'll be watching us from the bushes right now. They're not daft. They know when to make themselves scarce.'

Some time later, when things had calmed down, they ate a frugal picnic supper made out of all the scraps that Oscar, Dancer and Toffee had decided were not worth stealing. Suddenly Jim felt something wind itself around his leg.

'What a nerve, they're back and trying to soften us up!' Mum cried as Toffee curled herself around her neck, purring loudly. Oscar and Dancer were grovelling on their backs at Jim and Joe's feet, waving their substantial stomachs in the air to be tickled.

'Well,' said Mum. 'You can't be cross with them for long. We'll just have to keep a close eye on them.'

Oscar, Dancer and Toffee had a wonderful holiday. They were the toast of the campsite and everybody made a great fuss of them, even when they went off on dangerous hunting expeditions for other people's burgers and milk.

'We'll bring them back again,' said Mum. 'But next time we'll put a padlock on the fridge!'

ON THE ROAD

How far?

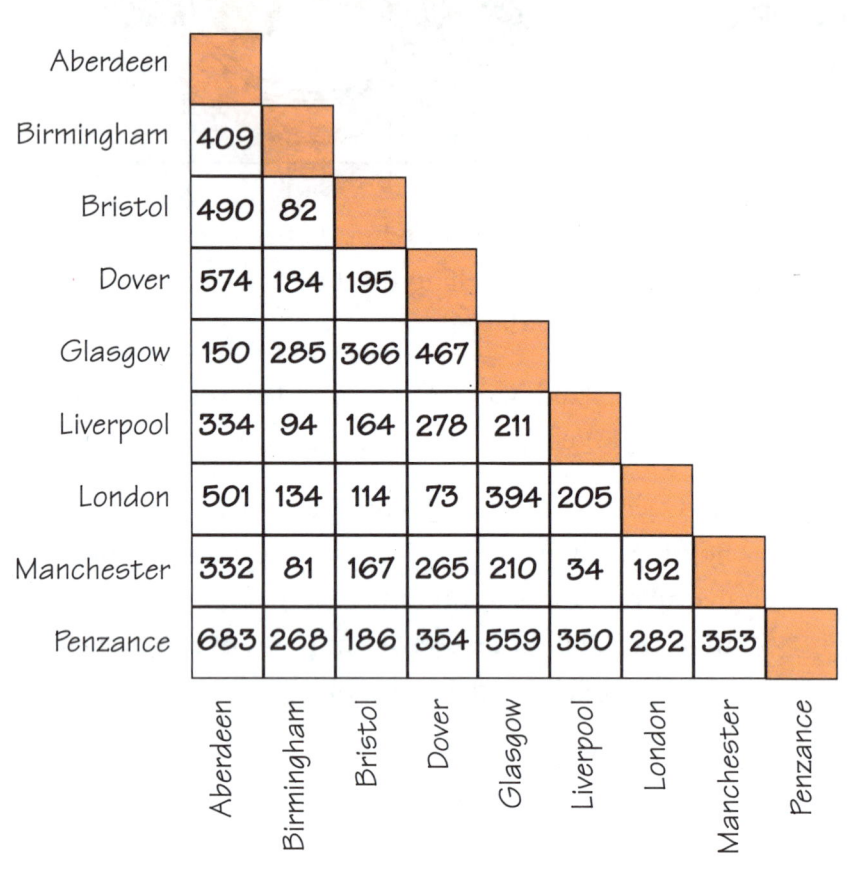

	Aberdeen	Birmingham	Bristol	Dover	Glasgow	Liverpool	London	Manchester	Penzance
Aberdeen									
Birmingham	409								
Bristol	490	82							
Dover	574	184	195						
Glasgow	150	285	366	467					
Liverpool	334	94	164	278	211				
London	501	134	114	73	394	205			
Manchester	332	81	167	265	210	34	192		
Penzance	683	268	186	354	559	350	282	353	

Distance

To find the distance between two towns or cities, such as Glasgow and London, just read across and up from their names on the axes. Sometimes you will need to change their order.

1. How far is it from Liverpool to Bristol? ___164___ miles

2. How far is it from Dover to Manchester? _____ miles

3. Which of these four towns is nearest to Birmingham? _____

4. How far is it from there to Birmingham? _____ miles

5. Which is the furthest town from Birmingham? _____

6. How much further is it from Bristol to Manchester than it is from Bristol to Liverpool?

_____ miles

Delivery drivers

Roger's Rolls

Roger's Rolls is a bread company based in Dover.

Their van makes deliveries to London, Bristol, Birmingham and Manchester, and then returns to Dover.

1. Which is the shortest route it could take?

   _____

2. How far is the journey?

   _____

3. How much further would the longest route be?

   _____

Pete's Peat

Pete's Peat is a gardening firm in Birmingham.

Their van delivers to Aberdeen, Glasgow, Liverpool and Manchester, before returning to Birmingham.

1. Which is its shortest route?

   _____

2. Which is its longest route?

   _____

3. What is the difference between the longest and shortest routes?

   _____

Check it out

1. If Roger's Rolls and Pete's Peat used vans that used 1 litre of petrol every 5 miles, how many litres would each use on their shortest routes?

   Roger's Rolls _____ litres   Pete's Peat _____ litres

2. If the Roger's Rolls van drove at an average speed of 41 miles an hour, how many hours driving would its shortest route take? _____

3. The Pete's Peat van drives at an average of 31 miles an hour. How much time does it take to cover its shortest route? _____

Maths search

P	F	M	A	T	H	E	M	A	T	I	C	S
L	A	U	Z	E	R	O	O	D	E	A	U	U
U	C	L	E	N	G	T	H	D	N	A	B	B
S	E	T	K	I	T	E	C	I	D	N	E	T
S	I	I	E	L	G	N	A	T	H	G	I	R
N	A	P	O	I	N	T	R	I	E	L	N	A
O	T	L	F	L	A	H	C	O	N	E	U	C
I	A	E	Q	U	A	L	S	N	A	E	M	T
T	D	I	V	I	S	I	O	N	Q	D	B	I
A	A	H	E	E	Y	R	R	E	D	O	E	O
T	E	T	N	J	N	A	I	D	E	M	R	N
O	R	O	N	O	C	T	A	G	O	N	E	T
R	A	T	I	O	P	E	P	E	G	N	A	R

1. _____	21. _____
2. _____	22. _____
3. _____	23. _____
4. _____	24. _____
5. _____	25. _____
6. _____	26. _____
7. _____	27. _____
8. _____	28. _____
9. _____	29. _____
10. _____	30. _____
11. _____	31. _____
12. _____	32. _____
13. _____	33. _____
14. _____	34. _____
15. _____	35. _____
16. _____	36. _____
17. _____	37. _____
18. _____	38. _____
19. _____	39. _____
20. _____	40. _____

There are over 40 words that we use in maths hidden in the word square.

1. Look forwards, backwards, up, down and diagonally.

2. How many words did you find? _____

Spot the number

See how quickly you can spot the numbers 1 to 9, in order, on car number plates. Only one number can be taken from each number plate.

For example:

H241HAK	P142SJM	R348 HTE
1	2	3

Spot the number 2

This time the numbers only count if they are the first number on the number plate.

For example:

P142SJM	H241HAK	R348HTE
1	2	3

L131XYZ

R348HTE

Linkword

Can you continue this maths linkword? Each word must join up with another one.
Use the words you found in the maths search to start you off.

```
M A T H E M A T I C S
U   E           U
L E N G T H     B R A C K E T S
T       U       T
I       N       R
P       D       A
L       R       C
I       E       T
C       D       I
A               O
T               N
I
O
N
```

Targets

Note down the numbers from a car's number plate.

1. What is the largest number you can make from these?

2. What is the smallest number?

3. How close can you get to 20?

You must always use all 3 numbers.

Targets 2

You can play this on your own or with a friend. Agree on a 2-digit number, like 48. Choose a car, note down its numbers, and try to use them to get as close to the target as you can.

Time yourselves for 1 minute only.

DEUTSCH (GERMAN)

Work it out

Read this cartoon strip. Do you understand what everyone is saying?
The translations at the bottom of the page will help you.

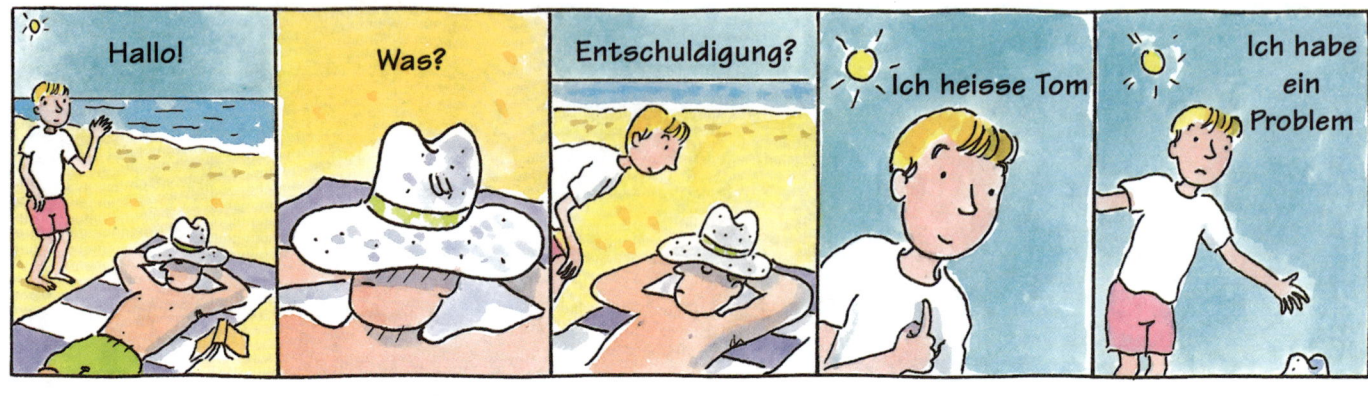

Wordbox

• Hello! • What? • Excuse me. • My name's Tom. • I've got a problem.
• Can you help me? • What's your name? • My name's Manfred. • How are you?
• Well, but... • Yes? • Your dog is sitting on my towel. • No! • Excuse me!

Test yourself

How many of these words do you understand?

Reis • Cola • Bröt • Apfel • Banane • Schokolade • Fisch • Nudeln • Wein • Kaffee • Limonade • Bier

Top tips!

German pronunciation is fairly easy.
Two things to remember are:

- ie – is pronounced '*ee*'
- ei – is pronounced '*i*'

Word families

Which of these languages look the same?

English	German	French	Spanish	Italian
1. one	eins	un	uno	uno
2. two	zwei	deux	dos	due
3. three	drei	trois	tres	tre
4. four	vier	quatre	cuatro	quattro
5. five	fünf	cinq	cinco	cinque

Linking numbers

Guess which word means which number.
Were you right?

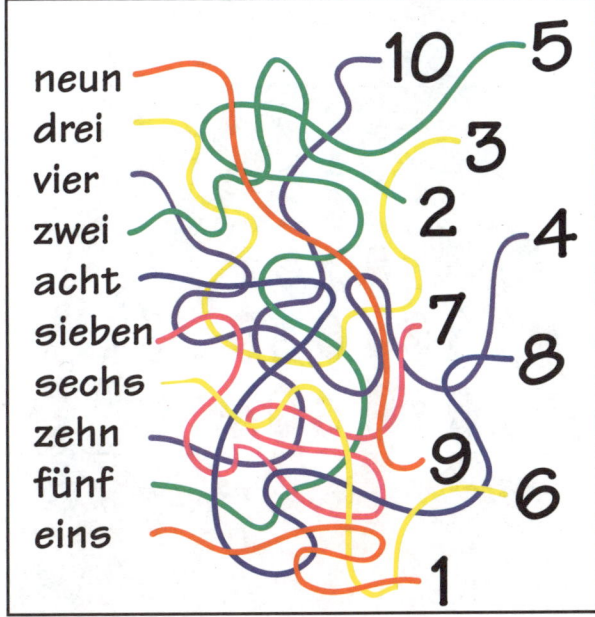

neun
drei
vier
zwei
acht
sieben
sechs
zehn
fünf
eins

10 5 3 2 4 7 8 9 6 1

SPORTY MATHS

Mr Pascal and the pinball machine...

```
      1
    1   1
  1   2   1
1   3   3   1
1   4   6   4   1
_ _ _ _ _ _ _ _
  _ _ _ _ _ _ _
_ _ _ _ _ _ _ _ _
```

This number pattern is named after a French mathematician called Pascal.

Can you fill in the gaps?

1. Add up the numbers in each row. Can you see a pattern? _____

2. Note down as many patterns as you can see. Look across and diagonally, in both directions.

3. Try drawing a triangle, this way up $\bigtriangledown$, around any 3 numbers e.g. $\overset{3\ 1}{\underset{4}{\bigtriangledown}}$.
   What do you notice? _____

   Does it always work? _____

Be a pinball wizard

The numbers on the pinball machine show the number of different routes to that point. There are 6 possible ways for the ball to end in the middle cup at the bottom, but only 1 way for it to end in each of the outer cups.

If you put £1.60 in the machine, at 10p a go, would you win or lose? _____

Would you finish with a profit or a loss? _____

By how much? _____

Remember that each go costs 10p. So a win of 20p is really only a win of 10p.

Decimal football

You will need to make a set of cards like those on the right and a ball and arrow like this:

0	0	0.25	0.5	0.75
1.25	1.5	2.25	2.5	2.75
3	3.5	3.75	4	4.5
5.0	5.25	6.25	Free Kick!	Free Kick!

1. Shuffle the cards and put them in a pile face down. Put the ball on the centre spot on the board.

2. Take it in turns to pick a card and move the ball towards your opponent's goal.

3. If you pick a FREE KICK! card, take 2 cards and play both together.

4. Make sure you call out the number you land on.

5. See if you can predict where you will land before you move.

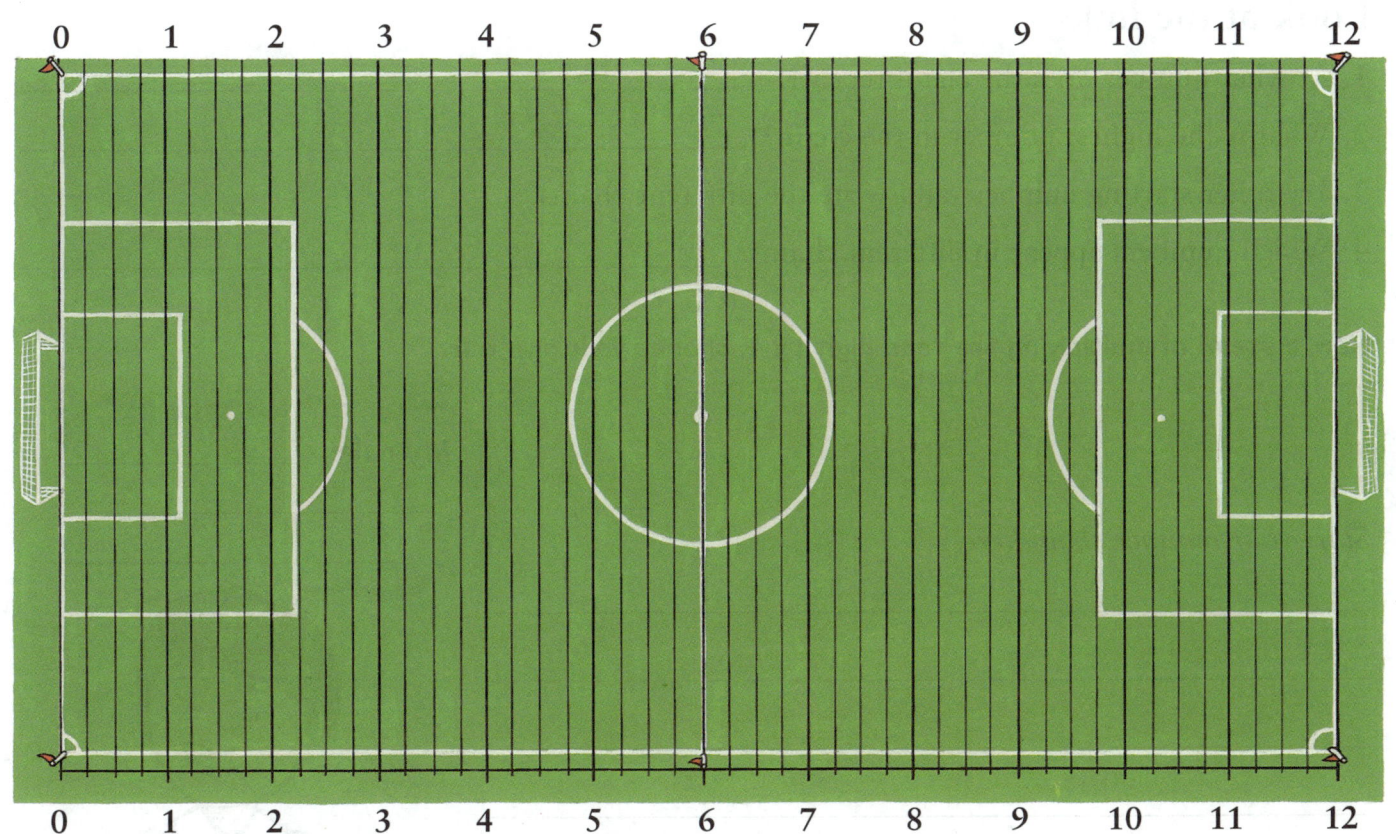

Try a new number line, perhaps 1–8 or 1–20. Make some different cards.

You could also make 'penalty' cards.

BRAIN POWER

Number chains

This is an example of a number chain.

1. Choose a 2-digit number.   **41**

2. Multiply the units digit by 4.   **1 x 4 = 4**

3. Then add the tens digit to the units.   **4 + 4 = 8**

4. If you carry on doing this you get **41 → 8 → 32 → 11**.

5. When you get to a single digit, like 8, just carry on, multiply the 8 by 4 and add the tens digit, 0, to give 32.

Carry on the number chain here

41 ⟶ 8 ⟶ 32 ⟶ _____

11 ⟶ _____

_____

_____

_____

41   **8**   **32**   **11**

Look at the links

1. At what number does the chain repeat? _____

2. What is the highest number in the chain? _____

3. Try other starting numbers and write the different chains.

4. Which numbers appear in different chains? _____

Now, instead of multiplying the tens digit by 4, choose your own rule.

Start your number chain here.

_____

_____

_____

_____

_____

My rule: _____
_____
_____

Mixed-up words

Match these words with their definitions.

Word	Definition
a) adjacent	a) pointing straight upwards
b) algebra	b) a slice of a circle that looks like a piece of cake from above
c) bisect	c) the point on a graph where the axes meet
d) congruent	d) a number multiplied by itself twice (e.g. 5 x 5 x 5)
e) cubic number	e) a point where two lines cross
f) digits	f) shapes that are identical in size and shape
g) ellipse	g) whole numbers that can be positive or negative
h) integer	h) this contains both a whole number and a fraction, like 3½
i) intersection	i) the result of a division operation
j) mixed number	j) this is equal to about 3.14. It is the relationship between the circumference of a circle and the diameter
k) origin	k) a number that only has two factors, itself and 1, like 3, 5 and 11
l) pi	l) a part of maths where letters can stand for numbers
m) prime number	m) to cut into two equal parts
n) quotient	n) something that can change its value
o) sector	o) symbols we use to write numbers, like 4, 3 and 7
p) variable	p) a corner of a shape
q) vertex	q) next to
r) vertical	r) an oval shape

Maths miscellany

Try this:

1. Pick a number.   7

2. Double it.   14

3. Add 5.   19

4. Multiply by 50.   950

5. If you have had your birthday already this year, add 1748.   2698

6. If you haven't had your birthday yet, add 1747.   2697

7. Subtract the year in which you were born.   2698 - 1987

You will be left with the number you started with and your age! 711

Now try it out on your friends.

THE WEATHER

The Great Storm of 1703

Fill in the gaps to complete this account of the Great Storm.

On Friday 26th November [1]_____, the [2]_____ storm
ever known hit Britain. During the [3]_____ terrible winds got up.
That [4]_____ they got worse. They [5]_____ and caused
havoc and [6]_____ throughout the [7]_____.
Hundreds of [8]_____ were wrecked or blown out to
[9]_____. Enormous [10]_____ battered the coast.
Rivers broke their banks and [11]_____ the countryside.
Farms [12]_____ destroyed and thousands of [13]_____ were
drowned. [14]_____ were blown off houses. Church [15]_____
collapsed. Winds reached [16]_____ of over 110 [17]_____ per
hour. [18]_____ were uprooted and windmills were overturned.

| trees | 1703 | miles | speeds | worst | spires | night | day | animals |
| flooded | waves | roofs | sea | ships | chaos | country | howled | were |

The Beaufort Scale

The Beaufort Scale is used to describe wind speeds. Fill in the parts that have been left out. Use the phrases at the bottom of the page to help you.

Force	Description	Wind Speed (miles per hour)	Signs
0	Calm	0–1	Smoke rises vertically
1	Light air	2–3	
2	Light breeze	4–7	Wind felt, leaves gently rustle
3	Gentle breeze	8–12	
4	Moderate breeze	13–18	Paper blown about
5	Fresh breeze	19–24	Small trees sway
6	Strong breeze	25–31	Branches move
7	Moderate gale	32–38	
8	Fresh gale	39–46	Small branches break off trees
9	Strong gale	47–54	
10	Whole gale	55–63	Trees uprooted, buildings damaged
11	Storm	64–75	
12	Hurricane	over 75	

Flags flutter

Chimney pots and roof tiles blown off

Havoc and disaster

Smoke slowly drifts

Whole trees move

Widespread damage

What's the weather?

Whether the weather be fine,
Or whether the weather be not,
Whether the weather be cold,
Or whether the weather be hot —
We'll weather the weather,
Whatever the weather,
Whether we like it or not!

Match these weather symbols to the correct descriptions.

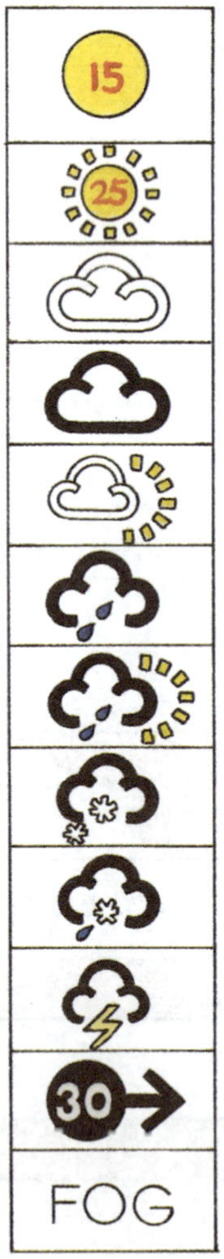

 **Sunshine** This yellow symbol stands for sunshine. The red number shows the temperature.

 **Fog** The word is written on the map where fog is expected.

 **Thunderstorm** A black cloud with yellow flash shows that there might be thunder and lightning.

 **Sunny intervals** The sun and cloud together stand for a mixture of sunshine and cloud.

 **Sleet** The cloud, snow and rain symbols stand for sleet.

 **Snow** The white flakes below the black cloud show snow.

 A black cloud stands for thick clouds and dull weather.

 **Wind** The black symbol shows wind direction. The white figure shows the speed in miles per hour.

 **Cloud** A white cloud stands for thin and patchy clouds.

 Rain The dark blue drops beneath the black cloud stand for rain.

 **Showers and sunny intervals** The cloud, rain and sun symbols stand for some showers and some sunshine.

Temperature
a Red figures on a yellow background stand for temperatures above freezing.
b Black figures on light blue show temperatures below freezing.

If you are not sure, watch a TV weather forecast.

Write your own forecast

Imagine you are giving a weather forecast for the map above. What will you say?

Script for weather forecast

SAFARI

I was floating around in a warm, dark place, tumbling over and over, with a terrible rumbling in my ears. I'd been gobbled up! The huge bull elephant had got me!

'Wake up! Wake up!'

I fought through the haze and opened my bleary eyes to see my friend Jake standing over me.

'You were thrashing around and muttering and grinding your teeth! What on earth's the matter, Nick? You must have been having a terrible nightmare.'

I peered around me, seeing the tent and remembering where I was, right in the middle of the bush in Kenya. I could hear the rustling of small creatures outside the tent, and the birdsong (I hoped) was deafening.

'Come on, you two,' said a voice from outside. 'Get your boots on. I want to check on the elephants. The wardens said they heard gunfire to the north last night.'

I grabbed a bottle of water and rushed out of the tent, tripping over my bootlaces. When Uncle Peter said, 'Move!' you moved, or he went without you. There was no way I was going to miss this. Uncle Peter was a scientist studying the elephants in the reserve. I want to do the same when I grow up. My name is Nick, by the way, and Uncle Peter is my mother's little brother.

We felt better once we were off. There was me, Uncle Peter, Jake and Julius, one of the wardens. We bounced over the rough track, avoiding anthills, warthog holes and the occasional rock.

'What happened last night, Julius?' asked Uncle Peter.

'Some of the team were on patrol and they saw lights, and were fired at. It's those poachers again – they'll be after ivory. I just hope that they were scared off by the patrol.'

We moved north, going more slowly as we reached the river. We were looking for the small herd, a family really, which Uncle Peter was studying. They all had names. Mzee was the big bull elephant. In Kenya, old men were called Mzee as a term of respect. He had several wives, including Big Bertha, the queen of the herd. The others were Speedy, because she was always last, Rumbletum, because it did, and Madonna, who was young and flirty. Rumbletum had two bull calves, Marks and Spencer.

'Let's stop here,' said Uncle Peter. 'Ssh! If we're quiet we may hear them eating.'

We sat still and soon we could hear movement, but it was different from usual. Suddenly the elephants crashed into the clearing, and we could see that Mzee was hobbling badly, a horrible metal trap caught round one of his back legs.

'It must be the poachers,' said Uncle Peter. 'Radio the camp, Julius, and get the others here. Thank goodness they didn't shoot him and steal his tusks.' The other elephants crowded round Mzee to protect him. They seemed to recognise the car and the friendly faces. After all, Uncle Peter had spent hours and hours with them as they moved through the bush.

We sat there quietly waiting, hoping that help would come soon, when suddenly Julius grabbed me by the arm.

'Nick,' he said, 'Can you hear that? It sounds like a truck in low gear down by the river. I'll go and have a look. You lot had better stay here. You're well hidden where we are. At least I've got my gun.'

Julius was a famous tracker. We knew that if anybody could spy on the poachers without being seen, it was him. I just hoped that they were not going to find us first.

After a few long minutes, which seemed like hours, Julius was back. 'They're stuck in the river,' he whispered. 'They have an ancient lorry and it is bogged down. What you heard was them revving it up as they tried to get out. I think that they are too busy to think about us. There are hippos in that pool and they are pretty bad-tempered. That patrol of ours is taking its time to get here!'

Through the bush I saw the rest of our team appearing stealthily on foot, rifles at the ready.

'We've got the dart gun for Mzee,' said their leader. 'We can tranquillise him and get that thing off his leg.'

'No!' whispered Uncle Peter. 'Be quiet! The poachers' lorry is stuck in the river. You must have scared them off last night and they're trying to make a run for it. I think we need to get them first. It will be such a pleasure to catch these killers. They've hacked so many elephants to bits for their ivory.'

'Right,' said Julius. 'Follow me. When we get near the river bank, spread out. The bank is high and we'll have a good vantage point. Edge up to it on your stomachs and lie flat. You two!' he said, pointing to a couple of wardens, 'Slip upriver a bit and get on the other side of them. It's them or us! Let's go!'

'Not you two, Nick and Jake!' said Uncle Peter. 'Your mothers will be furious when they hear about this. Stay here with the elephants. If anything goes wrong, hide in the bush and use the other radio to call for help.'

Off they went. We gave them five minutes, then Jake and I couldn't resist it any longer. We had to follow. Besides, the elephants were moving towards the river too and, after all, we were supposed to be protecting them.

We crawled forward as we got nearer to the riverbank, and saw the poachers, struggling to free the lorry. The more they tried, the more the engine whined, and there was a strong smell of burning rubber. To our horror, we could see two of the men, one with a rifle, climbing the bank towards where Julius lay hidden. The other two were knee-deep in water. They didn't notice that in the deeper part of the pool were the protruding ears and nostrils of several hippos – large, angry hippos who did not like strange, noisy beasts in their pool.

Suddenly, the world went mad. As the poachers climbed the bank, Julius took a shot at the man with the gun, blowing it out of his hand. The force sent the man tumbling backwards into the river where the hippos were waiting. Suddenly Big Bertha appeared and took care of the other man, crashing towards him as he stood paralysed with fright. It was as if she knew that these were the men who had killed her friends and wounded Mzee. She lifted her trunk, and with a fearsome bellow she pushed him over the drop and into the river below.

The other two poachers weren't doing much better. In front of them was Big Bertha and behind them were the wardens, while all around them were the angry hippos. They were soaking wet, exhausted, and absolutely terrified.

'Right!' said Uncle Peter. 'Let's round this lot up.'

The wardens, led by Julius, tied the men to a tree. Big Bertha stayed there, swinging her trunk and flapping her ears. The men were begging to be taken away.

Finally, the truck was driven up and the prisoners were loaded into the back. 'Next time we see them will be in court,' said Uncle Peter. 'They'll get twenty years each.'

'Right,' said Julius. 'Now that's over, where's Mzee?' He was hiding in a clump of trees, surrounded by the rest of his family. 'I think we'd better give him a little time to calm down,' said Uncle Peter. So we stayed quietly with the elephants, munching biscuits.

'I think we should get on with it now,' said Uncle Peter. 'We want to get it done today, and there's just enough time before dark. I just hope that Big Bertha and the others don't take it the wrong way. They've been through quite a lot in the last twenty-four hours.'

Julius and Uncle Peter took a canvas bag out of the car and laid the contents out on the bonnet. There was a dart gun, a bottle of tranquilliser and some instruments which looked more like large pliers.

The elephants were was standing quietly, swinging their trunks and flapping their ears gently. Mzee held his sore foot off the ground and let out a big elephantine sigh.

'Right,' said Julius. 'I'll walk up to him, and the rest of you cover me.' He took aim, fired and Mzee crumpled slowly in a heap.

'Quick!' said Uncle Peter. 'Let's do it!'

The wardens took the pliers and a metal cutter and removed the snare. Quickly, Uncle Peter put ointment on the wounded leg while Big Bertha and the others snorted restlessly in the background.

Fortunately, the wound was not as bad as they had feared. They all watched from a distance until Mzee got up groggily and stood swaying while the rest of the herd gently blew at him with their trunks.

'What a day!' said Uncle Peter. 'You'll have to tell your friends all about this.'

'Nobody will believe us,' we said. 'They'll think we made it all up.'

certificate

This is to certify that

_____

will be the **biggest** brainbox

in **Year 7.**

NOTES TO PARENTS

About your child

Your child will be:

• looking forward to secondary school;

• excited about meeting new friends;

• studying subjects which are the same as in the primary school but working from different programmes of study;

• beginning a modern foreign language such as French, German or Spanish;

• expected to behave responsibly, arrive for lessons on time and have the right equipment;

• anticipating more homework.

Introduction

This is a very exciting time for your child. Seven years of primary school have come to an end and the next phase of his or her education is about to begin. Visits to the secondary school will already have been made, during the previous term, so that first impressions of what to expect will already have been formed. Your child will probably have met some of the teachers and the form tutor and will know many of the other young people going to the school.

Although there will be much excitement about, for example, the new facilities offered by the gym, science laboratories or computer suite, there may also be some anxiety about the size of the school and the number of new people to get to know. Will I get lost? What happens if I'm late? Will I get detention if I forget my homework? These are some of the common concerns. Talking about hopes and fears will ensure that your child feels supported in the early weeks in the new environment.

Children may think there will be unpleasant initiation ceremonies. Whilst many realise that these are myths, some have genuine concerns about them. So it's important to offer reassurance.

Children need to have strategies for coping in school and you can help by talking about how to deal with different situations.

Make sure that the summer holiday provides your child with complete relaxation and refreshment as well as preparation for the adventure ahead. Have fun exploring new places together and look for opportunities to reinforce knowledge, skills and understanding that will be useful next year.

Stages of learning in the secondary school

Age	Year	Statutory assessment
11-12	7	
12-13	8	
13-14	9	Key Stage 3 National Tests
14-15	10	
15-16	11	External examinations, including GCSE
16-17	12	
17-18	13	External examinations, including A-Level and GNVQ

What to expect next year

Your child will probably be placed in a tutor group which meets for registration each day, and is likely to remain in this group for several subjects. Discussions held with staff from the primary school and information from records transferred from there may have influenced the make-up of these groups.

For subjects such as English and mathematics, and possibly science, your child may be placed in a set based on attainment in primary school. Some schools use entry tests to make these decisions but, where there are good curriculum links between primary and secondary schools, this is not usually found to be necessary.

If children have had some experience of accepting responsibility and organising themselves, they soon become accustomed to following a timetable, getting to know the expectations of teachers and carrying the necessary books and equipment from room to room for lessons.

The Curriculum

The curriculum in the first three years of the secondary school is based on the Key Stage 3 programmes of study of the National Curriculum. The inclusion of modern foreign languages (MFL) into the curriculum means that there is a total of eleven subjects to study. The choice of language varies between schools and may be influenced by teachers' language expertise.

Each subject will follow a scheme of work which has been agreed by each department and many will have a course textbook which the children will use. In some schools, textbooks have to be shared so they may not be readily available for use at home.

Some lessons, particularly in practical subjects, may be taught to half the year group at a time to improve access to facilities, but all pupils should be offered the same experiences.

All children should be given necessary support from teachers and some with special educational needs may receive additional help from an assistant in class. Teaching should take account of what children already know and understand. This should mean that children are not expected to repeat work that has already been covered at primary school.

Homework is usually set in accordance with an agreed timetable so that children have different subjects to deal with on different evenings. In this first year of secondary school, this is not usually too time-consuming so if your child experiences problems with overload, you should talk about it with someone at school. Children and parents need to be clear about what is expected.

Assessment

There are no statutory National Tests in Year 7. However, as in each year of the primary school, teachers are required to assess children's achievement and progress regularly to ensure that appropriate work is planned to meet their needs.

It is likely that children will experience more frequent assessments in the secondary school. These are often set at the end of a series of lessons, perhaps every two or three weeks. Children are usually, though not always, told when these will take place and homework is sometimes used for revision in preparation for a test. Children need feedback about their work to identify what they have done well and highlight where and how they need to improve.

Home and school together

As children get older and enter secondary school, parents often feel that it is increasingly difficult to support their work in school. This may be because the child resists what they see as adult interference or it may relate to parents' uncertainty about exactly what they can do to help. It is important to keep in touch with your child's teachers and respond to every opportunity to discuss progress.

Annual reports should give you information about progress and attainment in each subject, highlighting strengths and weaknesses, and should also include targets for improvement. However, as these are usually written in the summer term, it is important to try to have some contact with the school before this time to find out how your child has settled and what you may need to do to support him or her.

Most schools use a homework diary in which all homework is recorded and some request that parents sign these regularly to show that they have read them. Some schools use home-school contracts to show agreement between the teachers and parents about support for the child. These can really help to ensure that everyone is clear about what is expected and they demonstrate to the child that home and school are working together.

Make sure you are aware of the school's policy on homework. Plan with your child how to balance homework with other commitments, such music lessons, gym or time with friends. Decide when and where homework will be completed, ensuring the support of a comfortable working atmosphere. Take an interest in your child's work and offer constructive comments.

Helping your child

The summer should provide opportunities for children to extend their knowledge, skills and understanding. Every day creates situations that require the adaptation of existing knowledge to solve problems.

Spend some time thinking about the opportunities that the things you have planned might create, taking account of those things you feel your child should practise. In reaching decisions about what to do, you may like to consider including some of the activities on page 60.

Introducing a new language

Are you travelling abroad this summer? Use the opportunity to introduce your child to other languages.

- If you are travelling where French, German or Spanish is spoken you will be able to try out some of the phrases in this book.

- If you are travelling elsewhere abroad, get hold of a phrase book in that country's language so that you can try out some simple phrases.

- Even if it's not a language your child will meet in school, it will be fun. It should inspire confidence in speaking another language and will introduce new language structure and intonation.

Note-taking and speed writing

- Children often adapt more readily to secondary school if they have developed an easy, flowing writing style and understand how to write notes. Create situations during the summer to practise these skills, for example using books, video or CD ROM to research a place you will be visiting.

- Remind your child that in note-taking there is no need to write sentences — only key points need to be noted down.

Count and discount!

Good mental recall of number facts and the ability to 'figure out' are important numeracy skills which should be developed.

- Number games are fun and help to develop these skills, which are needed in real-life situations.

What's the question?

In the following examples, answers to problems are given and the child has to suggest an appropriate question, for example:

- The product of two numbers is 64. Several questions are possible but they must involve multiplication, for example: What is the product of 2 X 32? What is 4 X 16; 8 X 8...?

- The difference between two numbers, each greater than 50 but less than 100, is 16.

- The answer is half of 100.

- Make up examples of your own and encourage your child to suggest some too. They can be easier or harder to suit your child's level of attainment.

A day at the sales

This provides an opportunity to work with percentages. It can take place while out shopping or can be carried out as an activity at home.

- Look at discounts in shop sales. Some shops may offer 10% or 20% off goods. Others may advertise such things as '50% off all items on this rail'.

- Look at the original prices and help your child to calculate the reduced price. Talk about the ways to work it out without using a calculator.

- Make up some examples at home and do the calculations on paper.

- Discuss the relationship between one tenth and 10%; a fifth and 20%; 50% and a half.

Fuzz buzz!

This game, which is an advanced version of the game 'Fuzz' in Book 6, is for two or more players. It encourages knowledge and quick recall of multiplication facts.

- Players take it in turns to say a number in sequence, for example, the first says '1', the next '2', the next '3' and so on.

- The player whose turn it is to say 5 or any multiple of 5, for example, 10, 15, 20... must instead say 'fuzz'.

- When a 7 or multiple of 7 is reached, instead of saying '7', the player must say 'buzz'.

- When a multiple of 5 and 7 is reached, for example, 35 or 70, the player must say, 'fuzz buzz' !

- The result is as follows : 1, 2, 3, 4, fuzz, 6, buzz, 8, 9, fuzz, 11, 12, 13, buzz, fuzz, 16, 17, 18, 19, fuzz, buzz, 22....!

- A variation to increase difficulty is to reverse the order of play each time 'buzz' is said.

- Players are out if they say 5, 7 or any multiples of these numbers instead of the words 'fuzz', 'buzz' or 'fuzz buzz'. The winner is the last person left in the game.

- You can make up your own versions of this game using different words in place of chosen multiples.

Extending reading

A wide range of reading should be enjoyed throughout the holiday and different types of books, authors and styles of writing should also be encouraged.

NOTES ON USING THIS BOOK

Sources from history pages 4-7

Skills:

- Extracting information from sources
- Sequencing sources
- Analysing primary and secondary sources
- Distinguishing fact from opinion and looking for bias

Answers:

page 5: 1. low; 2. 'so poor and wretched'; 3. no (apart from the fact that the Britons fought against the Romans); 4. gold and silver; 5. C, D, E, A, B

page 6: 1. C, D, E; 2. A, B.
1. opinion; 2. fact; 3. fact; 4. fact; 5. opinion; 6. opinion.

page 7: 1. Suetonius; 2. Velleius; 3. Suetonius; 4. Velleius.

Advice to parents:

1. Extracting relevant information from sources is important for understanding the society of a time. Sequencing these sources is a basic historical skill. You may need to explain to your child how the dating system BC and AD works (dates before and after the birth of Jesus Christ).

2. Cicero (C and D) was writing at the time of Caesar's invasion; Caesar (E) was writing an eye-witness account soon after. But Plutarch (A) and Dio Cassius (B) were writing much later, basing their accounts on earlier writings.

3. Confusingly, a piece of writing can be both a primary and a secondary source, depending on how it is used. Plutarch is a primary source for his own period, but for the earlier period of Julius Caesar he is a secondary source.

4. Telling the difference between a fact and an opinion is another basic historical skill.

5. The first source, written while Tiberius was alive, is likely to be less reliable than the second. If Tiberius was a wicked ruler, no writer could have said this while he was living as a Roman emperor could kill writers whose books offended him.

6. Bias often affects the reliability of a source. Historians have to look at both sides of any question, weighing up the evidence.

Français (French) pages 8-9

Skills:

- Using and understanding basic French terms
- The ability to communicate in everyday contexts

Advice to parents:

1. Pronunciation is more important than spelling at this stage, and repetition is the key to success.

2. Repeat the game on a regular basis for practice.

3. Encourage your child to think of different ways to remember words and phrases.

4. It is important that you and your child take a 'have-a-go' attitude to speaking French, and play with the language as much as possible to feel more confident.

Detective work pages 10-13

Skills:

- Visual memory
- Reading and answering questions
- Sequencing pictures and writing a report
- Using logic and reasoning
- Using alternative symbols to communicate meaning

Answers:

page 10: 1. 3; 2. Biggs bank; 3. red; 4. a baker's van; 5. Sid's café; 6. 3; 7. yes; 8. no; 9. yes; 10. pushing a pram.

page 13: MEET ME TONIGHT UNDER THE OLD WOODEN BRIDGE. MAKE SURE YOU ARE NOT FOLLOWED. REMEMBER TO BRING THE SECRET PAPERS.
MEET ME TONIGHT.

Advice to parents:

1. Discuss how eye-witnesses are often unreliable because their memories play tricks on them.

2. Look at and discuss each 'photo' with your child. Use the visual clues to reconstruct the sequence of events, and number the photographs accordingly.

3. The secret code story is from ancient Greece and is based on one of the many inter-city wars at the time. Discuss the story and the coded message, and consider how else codes may be used.

4. Children are fascinated by secret codes. However, encourage your child to be systematic and patient when cracking the code. Discuss the fact that spy codes are sometimes so complicated they might take months to crack.

At the travel agent pages 14-17

Skills:
- Handling data
- Addition of times
- Understanding currency exchange

Answers:

page 15: 1. 3 hrs 30 mins; 2. 3h 45m; 3. 5h 30m;
4. 2h 45m via Munich.
A. 4h 30m; B. 8h 20m; C. 8h 20m.
1. Rome; 2. Madrid and Munich; 3. Athens, Munich and Paris.

page 16: 1. £9; 2. £5.50; 3. £24; 4. £60; 5. FF 200;
6. FF 500; 7. £8.50.

page 17: 1. £8; 2. DM 19.6
1. £6; 2. 1920 pesetas.
£1 = FF 9 so £12 = FF 108; £1 = $2 so £16 = $32; £1 = 200 pesetas so £9 = 1800 pesetas.

Advice to parents:

1. Adding time is difficult for many children because minutes are grouped in 60s rather than 10s, so take time to explain the methods to your child.

2. Investigations (like investigating these routes) are an important feature of secondary school mathematics.

3. Pages 16-17 introduce your child to conversion graphs. Different exchange rates can be used simply by altering the rate on the horizontal axis.

Our language pages 18-21

Skills:
- Understanding that language is not static
- Reading and following instructions
- Word matching
- Reading poetry
- Vocabulary extension and development
- Using homophones (words that sound the same)

Answers:

page 18: This picture shows a Native American.

page 21: 1. T; 2. F; 3. T; 4. F; 5. F; 6. T; 7. F; 8. F; 9. T;
10. F; 11. T; 12. F; 13. T; 14. F.
1. sale; 2. whole; 3. pane; 4. course; 5. horde.
1. allowed, aloud; 2. scent, sent; 3. stare, stair;
4. peace, piece; 5. bored, board.

Advice to parents:

1. Discuss with your child how our language is constantly changing, with new words developing e.g. astronaut, computer, video.

2. Have fun reading and discussing the poem, pointing out the trickiness of our language. If your family also speaks another language, discuss unusual words in that language.

3. Encourage your child to check the meanings of unfamiliar words in a dictionary.

4. Homophones are words that sound alike but are spelt differently and have different meanings. Mistakes with many of these words are common. Encourage your child to check the spelling and meaning of the words in a dictionary if he or she is unsure.

European tour pages 22-23

Skills:
- Knowledge of the map of Europe
- Identifying features of Europe
- Using coordinates

Answers:

page 22: Italy; UK; France; Germany; Spain.
1. 9.5cm - 1,425km; 2. 8.2cm - 1,230km;
3. 16cm - 2,400km; 4. 2.5cm - 375km;
5. 6.2cm - 930km

page 23: Lake District - UK; Eiffel Tower - France;
Parthenon - Greece; Leaning Tower - Italy;
Alhambra - Spain; Little Mermaid - Denmark;
The Alps - France/Italy/Switzerland.

Advice to parents:

1. The map scale is 2 = 300 km (1 cm = 150 km). Your child should use the coordinates to find the location of the postcards.

2. You could buy some blank postcards for children to make their own, illustrating them with European scenes. Use reference books to help you.

Español (Spanish) pages 24-25

Skills:
- Using and understanding basic Spanish terms
- The ability to communicate in everyday contexts

Advice to parents:

1. Pronunciation is more important than spelling at this stage, and repetition is the key to success.

2. Repeat the game on a regular basis for practice.

3. Encourage your child to think of different ways to remember words and phrases.

Sarah pages 26-29

Skills:
- Reading fiction in the first person
- Awareness of others

Advice to parents:

Discuss the story with your child. Does he or she recognise the character types? Use the story to start a discussion of friendships and bullying.

London's burning pages 30-33

Skills:

- Extracting information from maps and converting it into written text
- Extracting information from written historical sources
- Interpreting picture sources
- Detecting bias in historical sources

Answers:

page 30: 1. Because it was stopped by the river. 2. The greatest damage was caused on Tuesday.

page 31: 'It made me weep to see it'; 'horrid'.

page 32: 1. Buckets of water. 2. Using a fire-hook to pull down a building. 3. This is the last burning building in the row. By pulling down this building, they can stop the fire spreading. 4. They are praying to God to stop the fire. 5. Hand-squirts and gunpowder.

page 33: The lesson was that Catholicism was the true religion. 1. Against; 2. '...not one person turned to Heaven to ask for mercy. They only cursed their fate and grew more cruel.'

Advice to parents:

1. Extracting information from maps and converting it into written information is a useful skill for many subjects.

2. One reason to study a subject such as the Great Fire is to learn how people reacted to this disaster. Sources like Pepys' diary can show this.

3. A picture can hold as much historical information as a piece of writing.

4. Discuss the differences between various religious faiths with your child. Parallels can be drawn with modern situations e.g. of religious conflict.

5. The Dutch author had no way of knowing how everybody in London behaved during the fire – this source is Dutch propaganda. The Dutch wanted to persuade the Italians that the English were wicked and cruel.

Stowaways pages 34-37

Skills:

- Reading fiction
- Appreciating humour

On the road pages 38-41

Skills:

- Handling data
- Route finding
- Mental maths
- Maths vocabulary

Answers:

page 38: 1. 164 miles; 2. 265 miles; 3. Manchester; 4. 81; 5. Glasgow; 6. 3 miles.

page 39: Roger's Rolls: shortest route Dover-London-Bristol-Birmingham-Manchester-Dover; distance 615 miles; difference 257 miles. Pete's Peat: shortest route Birmingham-Liverpool-Glasgow-Aberdeen-Manchester-Birmingham; distance 1,256 miles; difference 388 miles.

1. 123 litres, 251 litres; 2. 15 hours; 3. 40.5 hours.

page 41: add, addition, angle, arc, area, cone, cube, data, dice, division, edge, equals, even, face, half, kite, length, mathematics, mean, median, mode, multiplication, net, number, octagon, odd, one, pair, pi, plus, point, range, rate, right angle, ratio, rotation, set, subtraction, ten, tenth, venn, zero (43 words).

Advice to parents:

1. The first activities help children to practise skills needed when travelling – reading mileages, finding routes and calculating speed and petrol consumption – which use and apply mathematics. Investigations are an important feature of secondary-level mathematics.

2. Pages 40-41 contain activities suitable for journeys which involve mental maths, observation skills and key words needed for maths.

Deutsch (German) pages 42-43

Skills:

- Using and understanding basic German terms
- The ability to communicate in everyday contexts

Answers:

page 43: Reis - rice; Cola - cola; Bröt - bread; Apfel - apple; Banane - banana; Nudeln - pasta; Schokolade - chocolate; Fisch - fish; Wein - wine; Kaffee - coffee; Bier - beer; Limonade - lemonade.

Advice to parents:

1. Pronunciation is more important than spelling at this stage, and repetition is the key to success.

2. As you read the picture story, play one character each and read the words out loud. German words sound pretty much as they look.

3. Encourage your child to think of different ways to remember words and phrases.

4. It is important that you and your child take a 'have-a-go' attitude to speaking German, and play with the language as much as possible to feel more confident.

Sporty maths pages 44-45

Skills:

- Investigating with numbers
- Mathematical vocabulary
- Working with decimals on a number line

Answers:

page 44:   1 5 10 10 5 1,
                1 6 15 20 15 6 1
              1 7 21 35 35 21 7 1
              You would lose 80p.

Advice to parents:

1. Your child needs to spot and continue number patterns when predicting the outcome of playing this pinball game.

2. The decimal football game will develop your child's understanding of decimal numbers, including tenths and hundredths. While most children are able to add and subtract decimals in sums, they are often unsure how decimals work as numbers in their own right. Modify the game by using a different number line or set of cards.

Brain power pages 46-47

Skills:

- Investigating with numbers
- Key mathematical vocabulary

Answers:

page 46:   41 → 8 → 32 → 11 → 20 → 2
              → 8 → 32 → 11 etc
            1. 8; 2. 41.

page 47:   a-q; b-l; c-m; d-f; e-d; f-o; g-r; h-g; i-e; j-h; k-c; l-j; m-k; n-i; o-b; p-n; q-p; r-a.

Advice to parents:

1. The number chain requires children to investigate the effect of applying a particular rule to numbers. It is an open-ended activity to help your child explore number patterns by trying different starting points, predicting outcomes and finding general rules. Investigations are an important feature of mathematics at Key Stage 3.

2. The second activity allows your child to revise and learn the terminology that will feature in his or her future mathematics lessons.

The weather pages 48-51

Skills:

- Using context clues to fill in missing words
- Reading and interpreting information in grid form
- Reading and analysing a poem
- Using symbols to represent information
- Map reading
- Script writing

Answers:

page 48:   Suggested answers (your child may choose others): 1. 1703; 2. worst; 3. day; 4. night; 5. howled; 6. chaos; 7. country; 8. ships; 9. sea; 10. waves; 11. flooded; 12. were; 13. animals; 14. roofs; 15. spires; 16. speeds; 17. miles; 18. trees.

page 49:   Force 1 - Smoke slowly drifts. Force 3 - Flags flutter. Force 7 - Whole trees move. Force 9 - Chimney pots and roof tiles blown off. Force 11 – Widespread damage. Force 12 - Havoc and disaster.

Advice to parents:

1. Look at and discuss the picture as a starting point for the passage. Ask your child to read the passage and suggest sensible words to fill the gaps. If a word cannot be found immediately, tell your child to read on and come back to the missing word. Encourage your child to first fill in the words in pencil, then to read the passage through again completely. He or she should check that the meaning is clear and change any words that don't seem right before inking them in.

2. Wind speeds are finely graded on the Beaufort Scale. Look at the grid and discuss the ways in which the wind speeds are described. Encourage your child to look carefully at the wording of the missing statements.

3. Encourage your child to read the poem several times, enjoying the feel of the words. Discuss how you can tell from the language that the poem was written some time ago.

4. Look at each weather symbol and discuss how well it represents the type of weather. Discuss the features shown on the map. Can your child point to the various countries? Does your child know where you live and the rough position of the major towns and cities? Use an atlas if he or she is unsure of these. Discuss the compass and name the compass points shown.

5. Ask your child to decide what the weather conditions will be and draw the relevant symbols.

6. While writing the script, your child could first record the forecast. Listen to it and discuss improvements.

Safari pages 52-55

Skills:

- Reading fiction
- Imagining unfamiliar situations

Advice to parents:

This story makes a good starting point for a discussion of African wildlife. Your child could research elephants and other animals further at the library.